NEW

KIDSPACE
IDEA BOOK

NEW
KIDSPACE
IDEA BOOK

WENDY A. JORDAN

The Taunton Press

To my mother and my daughter, both inspirational

The Taunton Press, Inc., 63 South Main Street, PO Box 5506, Newtown, CT 06470-5506
e-mail: tp@taunton.com

Editor: Stefanie Ramp
Jacket/Cover design: Jeannet Leendertse
Interior design: Lori Wendin
Layout: Carol Petro
Illustrator: Christine Erikson
Front Cover Photographers: Top row, left to right: Photo courtesy Georgia-Pacific Corporation; Photo courtesy
Stephen Smith Images; Photo courtesy Wallies®; Photo © 2004 Scott Rothwall
Middle row, left to right: Photo © Anderson-Moore Builders, Inc., photo by Sharon Haege, Brick House Creative;
Photo courtesy California Closets; Photo © 2004 Scott Rothwall; Photo © www.antongrassl.com
Bottom row, left to right: Photo courtesy Steven W. Cook, Steven Cook Architecture; Photo © 2004 Chun Y. Lai;
Photo courtesy Vibel, www.vibel.com; Photo © 2004 Feinknopf Photography
Back Cover Photographers: Top: Photo © Laurence Taylor. Bottom, left to right: Photo courtesy The Land of Nod;
Photo courtesy York Wallcoverings; Photo © Taylor Dabney, Photographer

Library of Congress Cataloging-in-Publication Data

Jordan, Wendy Adler, 1946-
  New kidspace idea book / Wendy A. Jordan.
      p. cm.
  ISBN-13: 978-1-56158-694-3
  ISBN-10: 1-56158-694-3
  1. Children's rooms--Planning. 2. Interior decoration--Human factors. I. Title.
  NK2117.C4J674 2005
  747.7'7--dc22

                              2004019929

Printed in the United States of America
10 9 8 7 6 5 4 3

Acknowledgments

Writing this book was a pleasure, not only because of the joyful subject matter but also because I was assisted by so many talented people along the way.

The ingenious projects that fill these pages came from scores of creative designers, architects, remodelers, businesspeople, and homeowners. They generously shared their ideas, and I wholeheartedly thank them for enriching the book. I encourage readers to mine the credits section for the names of these talented people, all of whom know how to make kids' spaces great.

Experts in specialized design disciplines served as valuable resources during my research. I am most grateful to them. Included in this gallery of pros are Susan Arndt, Susan Arndt Interiors, Framingham, Mass.; William Asdal, CGR, Asdal Builders, LLC, Chester, N. J.; Theresa Bartolo, Allied Member ASID, Theresa Russell Interiors, Boca Raton, Fla.; Judy Gordon, Allied Member ASID, Judy W. Gordon Interior Design, Northbrook, Ill.; Jolayne Lyon Hawver ASID, Design Consultants Inc., Topeka, Kans.; Glenn Robins, TotallyCustomWallpaper.com, Atlanta, Ga.; Edie Twining, Monastero & Associates, Inc., Cambridge, Mass.; Scott Van Leer, Maurice Electrical Supply Lighting Designers, Rockville, Md.; and Larry Zimmerman, DGI-Invisuals, Burlington, Mass.

The editorial team at The Taunton Press provided an ideal mix of top-notch professionalism and friendly support. I thank Maureen Graney, Carolyn Mandarano, Wendi Mijal, and Stefanie Ramp for shepherding the project from brainstorm to bookshelf.

Finally, I want to thank two members of my family—my husband, Doug, who was constantly available to answer construction questions as my in-house consultant, and my daughter, Heather, who is my divining rod in discovering what kids like.

Contents

Introduction ▪ 2

Chapter 1
Bedrooms ▪ 4

Welcome Home, Baby ▪ 6

Toddler Territory ▪ 14

Grade School Districts ▪ 30

Perfect for Preteens ▪ 52

Teen Domains ▪ 70

Shared Spaces ▪ 76

Rooms That Grow Up ▪ 88

Chapter 2
Splashy Bathrooms ▪ 94

Extreme Themes ▪ 96

Accent Details ▪ 98

Using Every Inch ▪ 102

Grown-Up Baths ▪ 106

Chapter 3
Places to Play,
Places to Study · 108

Recreation Zones · 110

Setting the Scene · 116

Bonus Space · 118

Upstairs, Downstairs · 122

Clutter Control · 128

Homework Zones · 134

Chapter 4
Outdoor Play Spaces · 140

Dynamic Playhouses · 142

Active Outdoor Adventure · 148

Lighthearted Landscaping · 150

Credits · 152

Introduction

Kids' rooms are in a class by themselves. Other parts of the house may be designed with a certain reserve, but the most appealing spaces for children are those that are created with abandon and joy. Of course, there are implicit rewards in crafting an environment for children. We have the pleasure of shaping a setting that fosters both fun and learning, a place where kids can thrive and grow. And besides, we're all young at heart; designing rooms for kids draws on our own playfulness and youthful spirit.

I was impressed by that "fun factor" in kids' room designs when I collected ideas for the original *Kidspace Idea Book*. I'm

even more impressed by it now. The first book offered hundreds of excellent designs from around the country and beyond, and I was happy to learn that designers and homeowners alike found much inspiration in those pages. It was particularly gratifying to know that the book was used exactly as we had intended —as a source of ideas to build on and personalize rather than simply reproduce.

I began researching kidspaces again and discovered a whole new generation of wonderful designs, all of them fresh and vibrant. Those new designs are presented in this book. Some are big ideas—dream rooms, you might say. They are here to inspire, not intimidate. In fact, I've made a point of zeroing in on the specific ideas contained in these rooms so that you can apply them as a package or make à la carte selections. In either case, you can interpret the ideas as you wish and make them your own.

Other ideas are simpler but just as creative. I've highlighted many economical ideas, easy-to-implement techniques, and shortcuts to great designs. There is some-

thing for everyone in these pages: designs for kids of all ages; projects for do-it-yourselfers as well as those that may be best handled by professionals; approaches for whole rooms as well as room areas and components; off-the-shelf as well as custom solutions; clever built-ins as well as room-making accessories.

All the pieces are here. With a touch of your own imaginative spark you can combine them to create kidspaces just right for your needs.

Bedrooms

I t may be called a bedroom, but a child's room is, of course, much more than that. It's where the child sleeps and plays, where she dresses and studies, and where she can go to be with friends or spend some solo time. The best kids' bedrooms are shaped around all of these functions and around the kids themselves—their ages, interests, personalities, and imaginations.

The younger the child, the more simple the room should be. A toddler is happy with a few open toy bins at floor level, while most preteens need ample shelving and drawer space. A small child's room should have zones readied for crafts, games, and reading, as well as generous floor space for active play. Older children don't need such compartmentalized areas, but their rooms should still have at least three zones: for homework, for sitting with friends, and for sleeping.

Every child welcomes a place to relax or decompress. Reserve the quietest, coziest corner for that retreat, then structure the rest of the room around it. Platforms, two-sided cabinetry, and archways help define different zones, while lofts, nooks, pass-throughs, and secret hide-aways add intrigue.

There's no need to puzzle over a theme for the room. Ask your children; they'll know exactly what they want.

◀ WHIMSICAL HIGHLIGHTS, such as the picketed bed boards and the birdhouse bedposts and wall-mounted shelves, turn a practical bedroom into a secret garden. A palette of outdoorsy colors knits the room together. The jumbo window seat with under-bench drawers is one play center; the toy box and chair form another.

Welcome Home, Baby

THREE WORDS — *CELEBRATION, COMFORT, AND CHEER* — sum up a great nursery. Almost any room, no matter how small, becomes a joyful place for baby and parents when it is suffused with light and color and outfitted with a suite of coordinated furnishings and accessories.

For comfort and convenience, room arrangement is key. Place the crib away from drafts but near cheerful accents that can stimulate and entertain the baby. Store diapers and supplies out of sight but handy to the changing table, and include a comfortable chair in a warm, light spot for nursing and rocking your little one.

Before you know it, your baby will be a toddler. Ready the room for this by investing in sturdy, versatile built-ins and furnishings that have adjustable or replaceable components. And choose a decorative theme and colors that will keep their appeal at least until your child starts school. That, too, will come before you know it!

▶ AN ALLOVER WASH OF COLOR, a large, low skylight, and inconspicuous track lights infuse this small room with luminosity and life. The aqua-tinted, diamond-coat plaster forms a pleasing backdrop for toys and accents in primary colors, while the white trim and furnishings lend a sparkling contrast.

◀ ▲ THE PLAYROOM, ADJACENT TO THE BEDROOM SHOWN on the facing page, is a safe, welcoming place for infants and toddlers with its low-to-the-ground focus and soft carpet. Brightly colored surfaces and a skylight give the room a sunny, cheerful tone. The innovative shelving makes the best use of the low-angled ceiling while adding a touch of whimsy and big compartments for picture books and toys.

▲ FABRIC WALL COVERING establishes a soft, gentle, sound-insulated atmosphere. The painted ceiling and decorated wardrobe provide interesting images for the baby to survey when lying in the crib or being rocked in the chair.

OUTFITTING THE ROOM

▼ PLAN AHEAD WITH A SETUP LIKE THIS. When a diaper-changing area is needed, secure a changing station to the top of a 3-ft.- or 4-ft-high dresser. Once the station is outgrown, piggyback accessory drawers on the dresser top to gain extra storage.

▲ SIMPLE SHELVING FRAMES THIS CRIB and creates colorful display space. Dowels threaded through the shelving double as perches for stuffed animals and hanging rods for towels or receiving blankets.

◄ WITH ITS FENCE MOTIF, this radiator cover is more than a safety feature; it becomes a design asset, helping to create a lighthearted outdoorsy theme in the room. Several inches wider than the radiator, the cover also forms a convenient tabletop.

ARTISTIC TOUCHES

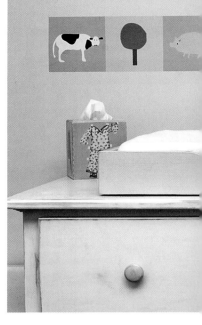

◄ THIS FRIENDLY CATERPILLAR
was painted close to the floor,
where it will entertain the baby
when he is playing on the rug.
A stencil, decal, or wallpaper
cutout would work just as well
if your artistic skills are shaky.

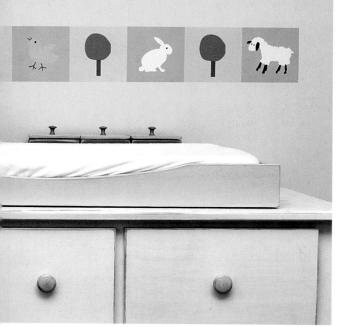

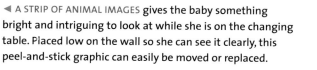 ◄ A STRIP OF ANIMAL IMAGES gives the baby something bright and intriguing to look at while she is on the changing table. Placed low on the wall so she can see it clearly, this peel-and-stick graphic can easily be moved or replaced.

▼ ► EVEN A ROOM WITH VERY FEW WINDOWS can be transformed into a sunny nursery. The soft glow of this basement room was achieved with rag-washed interior latex paint diluted with water. A few farmyard friends were added, as well as a topcoat of glaze that makes the walls washable.

READY FOR CHANGE

▶ FANCIFUL BUILT-INS AND PERKY COLORS create a joyful environment for a baby. But the room is prepared for a toddler, with generous play space, toy shelves, and a window seat. When the child reaches school age, the desk is ready and waiting.

▼ CALMING AND PLEASING FOR THE BABY, the soft colors, quiet patterns, and ceiling art in this room will remain appealing as the child grows. The changing table and bench will make easy transitions to a low dresser and a toy box respectively, both of which are accessible to a toddler or small child.

◄ INSTEAD OF A NURSERY that can be adapted for older kids, this is a grown-up room with the comforts of a nursery. The curtained niche is a cozy shelter for a crib or bed. The hanging couch—a Gloucester hammock—is a wonderful place to rock the baby now, but later it can be a guest bed or a place for kids to play or read.

Safety First

GET OFF TO A SAFE START with a child's room that's designed to prevent mishaps as well as reactions to allergens or chemicals.

Cover outlets and keep electrical cords out of reach. Drapery pull cords should have breakaway tassels and be kept beyond the reach of very small children. If you are using freestanding furniture, make sure that it is tip resistant and attach shelving firmly to the wall. Low corners on furniture should be rounded. Keep climbable furniture away from windows. Crib slats should be no more than 2⅜ in. apart—too small for a baby to squeeze her head through.

Volatile organic compounds (VOCs) can also be a problem, causing allergies and even illnesses. To avoid them, use natural or untreated materials, such as solid wood, formaldehyde-free fiberboard, and natural, non-permanent-press fabrics. Hardwood and linoleum are good flooring choices. Area rugs are easier to keep clean, but if you install carpeting, use solid rubber padding.

CIRCUMVENTING SAFETY HAZARDS, this room has shutters rather than drapery with pull cords and recessed lights rather than lamps with cords. The natural wool carpet is easy to vacuum, and the cotton rug is machine washable. Nontoxic ceramic tile covers the sill.

As for finishes, go with nontoxic paint, wallpaper, and wallpaper glue. Avoid putting vinyl wall covering on exterior-facing walls, as it can trap moisture that cultivates mold. After painting or papering, air out the room for a week or two before bringing in the furniture.

Toddler Territory

WHETHER ROLLICKING ON THE FLOOR, rolling a toy truck, or rapt in a storybook, toddlers are keenly engaged in every experience. A toddler's room should not only be a cheerful, enabling environment for these young adventurers, but it should also be part of the adventure.

Stow toys where they are easy for toddlers to see and reach, using a dynamic mix of colorful shelves and open bins. Add a storage/play structure shaped like a car, horse, caterpillar, or train. Turn the headboard into a shallow cote for stuffed animals.

Cover low walls with chalkboard or magnetic paint, attaching boxes full of jumbo chalk sticks and whimsical magnets. Cluster coloring books, puzzles, and skill-building games alongside a kid-size table and seats.

Reserve plenty of open floor space. Toddlers need room to run around, play with big toys, or stretch out on the rug. Just as important: a soft-surfaced, enveloping corner where kids can curl up and rest.

▼ IT IS POSSIBLE TO COMBINE a compelling theme with clear, open play spaces. This garden motif is bright and sprightly, with real fence posts, large paper flowers, and faux-painted grass, butterflies, and ladybugs. The sunny yellow wall is graduated in shade, expanding the sense of space by becoming lighter at the ceiling.

▲ AN UPWARD FOCUS AND LIGHT, airy images make this room feel open and cheerful. The fresh outdoor scene begins at midwall, making the room seem bigger, while the clouds on the overhanging ceiling define a snug bed niche. The friendly wall art offers a customized alternative to framed pictures.

◀ A JUMBO CHALKBOARD defines the play area of this room. Though framed for a finished look, it is actually painted directly on the wall with chalkboard paint. The navy wainscoting brings the focus of the room down to the toddler's level.

▲ BIG, BOLD SHAPES ARE EASY for small children to understand. Exaggerated sizes and forms give this transitional nursery–toddler room a fanciful, Alice-in-Wonderland quality. The low table is practical as well as fun, and the overscale knobs, easy for toddlers to handle, can be replaced later as the kids grow up.

◄ A DYNAMICALLY SHAPED ROOM can be as much fun as the toys it contains. Every curve, triangle, and corner of this room invites interaction, functioning as either a storage place or a play zone. The airplane bed with wing shelf turns the deep angle of the wall to advantage.

▲ A HOUSE IS ONE OF THE FIRST SHAPES kids recognize and is a perennial favorite with the younger set. The triangular roof shape of this wall transforms the whole room into a fun, kid-friendly space. The wall also tempers the bed's exposure to light and forms a display area. The space-saving cabinet echoes the triangle theme.

▶ INSPIRED NOTCHES—from the little bedside-wall cutouts to the window bay—give this room personality. A recess between built-in closets makes an inviting play niche. Hooks in the niche hold playthings now, but later the space can be used as a dressing area.

Quick and Easy Highlights

Looking for design ideas that are easy on the wallet and simple to implement? Try these.

- Garnish the walls with game boards or game pieces from your toddler's favorite games or with simple constructions made from colorful, flat building blocks.

- Ring the room with bright pegs or hooks at chair-rail height. They are both decorative and functional; use them to hang hats, souvenirs, blue ribbons, stuffed animals, framed pictures, or small shelves.

- Cut down the legs of an old table and coat it with glossy paint to craft a game table or hobby center.

- Line painted orange crates with quilted fabric. They make handy bins for toys, books, even socks.

- Spray-paint baskets of different shapes and sizes to hold everything from large toys to building sets to crayons. Baskets with handles can hang on wall hooks.

▼ TODDLERS LIKE OBJECTS THEY CAN TOUCH, so the bright cutout plywood octopus, submarine, and waves on this bed are perfect for a child who loves playing in the water. Automotive paint gives the cutouts a hard, durable surface. Toddlers also like personalized things, hence the undersea mural featuring his pet dog and cats.

FAVORITE THINGS

▲ BIG, COLORFUL PLANES AND CARS make this space-efficient suite of built-ins feel friendly for a toddler. Made of ³/₈-in. medium-density fiberboard (MDF), they can be removed when the child is older, leaving handsome cherry cabinetry with colorful veneer edging and wood knobs.

► THIS ROOM IS OUTFITTED WITH FUN, flexible furnishings including a fold-down play surface on the right that rests on an open drawer. The bus-themed bench/radiator cover encloses toy boxes. A foam mattress nests inside another with a foam ring; without the inner mattress, it works as a transitional bed for a toddler.

▲ WHAT CAN YOU DO if your child's bedroom is small but her doll collection is big? Build a dollhouse headboard with inset shelves. This plywood structure has three shelf levels and a dynamic array of windows.

Choosing Colors

WHAT COLORS ARE BEST for a child's room? The answer depends partly on the room and partly on the child's nature. Light colors expand space and darks lend intimacy. Cool colors such as blues and greens are soothing, while warm reds, oranges, and yellows are stimulating.

By age three or four, children have favorite colors. Be daring; use these colors to give their rooms a personal flavor. To find a winning palette, display crayons in the six primary and secondary colors (red, yellow, blue, orange, green, purple) and ask the child to choose her favorite. Next, ask for a second and third choice. Sort through more crayons or paint chips in related shades to refine the choices.

The least intense shade probably is best as the dominant room color. Use another favorite color for a third of the room's finishes, such as on molding or cabinetry. Top off the scheme with accents in the third tone. Before settling on colors, look at large paint swatches in the room throughout the day and evening and under different lighting to ensure the colors you choose stay true and appealing.

▲ A SIMPLE DEVICE—painting one wall yellow and the other blue—gives this room personality and verve. Drawers in a yellow and blue checkerboard play off the theme, as do the slide-out plastic toy storage bins in box frames.

BRIGHT IDEAS

▶ INSPIRATION FOR the colors and the graphics used in this room came from playful window-covering fabric. Cars, trains, and other painted images soar high on the wall and even on the ceiling, leaving wall space open for pictures. An oil or latex glaze gives the walls and ceiling a light, watercolor effect.

▲ THOUGH RELATIVELY INEXPENSIVE, the three-dimensional elements in this room add a magical touch. Leaves and apples cut from cloth hang on the painted tree and on actual tree branches arranged around the room. Lightly padded fabric shingles give dimensional heft to the awning. The curtain holdbacks are flowers made of cloth-covered wire.

▲ SHELVES BECOME THE HIGHLIGHT of the room when they look like something kids love. This mock tree house is a display surface for toys.

Style on a Shoestring

A SMALL BUDGET need not be a handicap. Instead, use it as the impetus for finding inventive design solutions. This toddler's room is as clever in design as it is in cost savings. Built-ins, "custom" furnishings, and the vibrant, outdoorsy theme bring energy and joy to an otherwise ordinary space. However, nothing about the room was expensive.

The rich colors were achieved with reduced-price latex semi-gloss paint that had been mixed wrong for previous customers. The cupboard doors are old shutters. The closet doors are old storm doors with fabric inserts. The patchwork-style bulletin board wall is composed of 12-in. cork squares wrapped in bright fabric.

Topped with green nylon netting, the chimney shaft becomes a leafy tree that adds dimension to the outdoor motif. Pillow stuffing glued to foam board makes puffy clouds. Speckled like a mushroom, the play table is painted plywood set on a paint-can pedestal. The chairs, which are fabric-wrapped paint cans half-filled with sand, come with handles for easy transport.

The steps to the upper bunk are built-in toy boxes crafted of 2x4s and plywood. As the toddler grows, his room can easily be repainted, and new furnishings can be bought or built as needed. The homeowners wisely purchased standard-size bunk beds, which will accommodate their boy throughout his childhood and adolescence no matter how fast he grows.

▲ THE VERSATILE CUPBOARDS and bulletin board wall are easy for a toddler to use, yet practical for a taller child.

▶ DOUBLE DOORS BLEND INTO THE LANDSCAPE of the room, disguising a large, practical closet with stacked rods and plenty of shoe space.

◄ A CLEVER PAINT JOB
brings the ceiling down
to a friendly height
for toddlers and
de-emphasizes the
asymmetrical window
placement. Whimsical,
free-form patio pavers
are painted on a
wood floor.

PLAY GROUND

◄ A LOW CEILING creates a cozy niche that will be a magnet for small children. To define the niche as a play space, everything—mirror, lamp, and bookshelves—is at toddler height.

▼ THE BOOKCASE PARTITION neatly organizes this room into sleeping and activity areas, leaving plenty of floor space for playing. Toy bins are accessible but behind cabinet doors to reduce clutter. The top bunk can be used for play space too, and the lamp-post makes fun lighting.

Montessori at Home

THE MONTESSORI SYSTEM—which is aimed at helping young children develop mentally, physically, and socially through learning in a nonre-strictive, kid-friendly environment— has a place at home as well as in the classroom. Montessori experts say young children learn by observing and voluntarily practicing skills. They also say that children up to age six function best in familiar, organized surround-ings where they can freely choose activities.

In a child's room, this means that tables and chairs should be kid-size and shelves for toys and books should be low, making it easy for kids to do what they want and find what they need. Toy bins should be labeled by picture, word, and/or color so that chil-dren can keep their playthings orga-nized. Same goes for clothing storage.

These strategies will help your child pick up skills, learn good habits, develop responsibility, and feel proud of her accomplishments.

CONTAINING THE FUN

▲ TO CAPTURE EVERY INCH of activity space, most of the storage in this bedroom—including "dresser drawers"—was moved into the closet. The only thing the kids will outgrow in this closet arrangement is the low hanging rod; it can be replaced or topped with a second rod as needed.

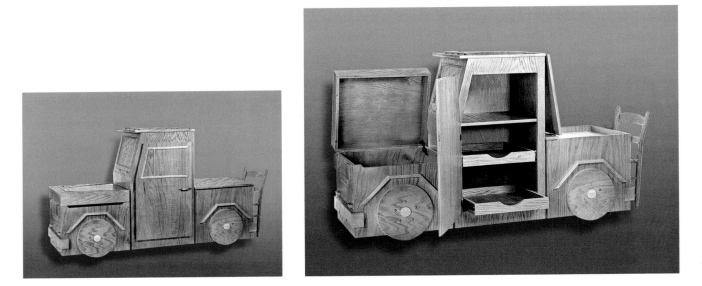

▲ AN IMAGINATIVE STRUCTURE like this adds both storage and play space. Kids can climb on the truck or play games on its tabletops. The storage sections include a toy box, large slide-out drawers with rims to keep toys from falling out, and a shallow desk compartment.

◄ WHEN SPICED UP with a cheery pattern or washed in a toddler's favorite colors, simple shelves or pegboards become fun to use.

► BENCH SHELVES keep books and toys visible yet put away. Another advantage is that they store things close to the floor where toddlers sit and play. The seat pad is easily replaced as kids grow and their tastes change.

▲ SPRINKLED ACROSS THE WALL, small storage cubes work as decorative accents and resting places for kids' stuff. To personalize them, line the boxes with bright paint, paper, or children's art.

▲ THE CLOSET DOOR becomes a playful and hardworking part of the room when it is decorated and fitted out with an array of racks, hooks, and bins for clothes and toys.

Grade School Districts

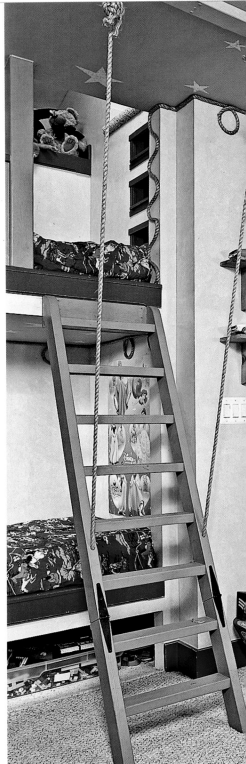

LIFE IS BIG AND BOLD for grade school children. They are making new friends, discovering new interests and activities, embracing the latest fads, and delighting in make-believe. That's why bold ideas are just right for a schoolchild's bedroom.

Bring on the jungle animals or dinosaurs, castles or butterflies, mermaids or cowboys. Go ahead with the vibrant colors and trompe l'oeil scenes. Go all out with canopy beds fit for princesses and mosquito-netted safari cots fit for little adventurers. Kids this age love surroundings drenched with atmosphere.

They also invest energy and enthusiasm in the sports and hobbies they've developed an interest in. Set up part of the room as a dedicated space for sports equipment, model plane projects, or jewelry making. Incorporate shelves and display walls around the room for handiwork, collections, posters, and prizes.

▲ HAVING A ROOM under the eaves is fun; having one with a dormer window and a cozy bed niche is even more so. White walls brighten the room while tinted ceilings lend intimacy, especially in the niche. Under-seat toy drawers and built-in bookshelves provide storage without absorbing floor space.

▲ SHEETS OF PERFORATED HARDBOARD can easily be cut to size to make a wall for displaying and stowing a child's belongings. Strong enough to support laden shelves, bins, and baskets, the panels also can hold pictures, movable hooks, and a changing exhibit of collectibles.

▲ A WILD WEST ROOM is a young boy's paradise. The life-size sheriff, horse-shoe hooks, and band of glued-on lasso rope express the theme energetically. But the adventure doesn't stop here. Inset steps from the upper bunk lead to a 12-ft. by 4-ft. fort that occupies surplus headroom. Ropes strengthen the bunk ladder; the bottom steps fold up to keep small children from climbing.

THEMES AND VARIATIONS

▲ THIS ROOM WILL BE SIMPLE to change when teams rotate in and out of interest and the sports fan grows older. The two-sided storage unit reinforces the "home" versus "visitor" team idea while making efficient use of space; its varied shelves accommodate assorted trophies. The cork scoreboard is big enough for posters and other memorabilia.

► CORRAL THE FRONTIER SPIRIT with lumberyard finds. This jailhouse headboard arrests attention with its shingled rooftop, shutters, and barred window. Rough-sawn planking along the wall is both evocative and functional, providing display shelves and tabletops. Crossed supports give the bed the rough and ready look of a cabin bunk.

▼ ◄ OVERHEAD ACCENT LIGHTING can energize a variety of themes, as these two bedrooms in the same house illustrate. In the castle room a ring of small, tinted lights raises the focus to the crenellations, heightening the illusion of being in a medieval tower. A dome dotted with fiber-optic lights in the other room recreates the orientation of the stars and planets on the child's birthday.

The Right Mix of Lighting

WITH GOOD LIGHTING, a child's room is safer and more pleasant to use. The room needs both overall ambient lighting and channeled task lighting. Decorative accent lights are icing on the cake.

Ceiling fixtures should illuminate the whole room, leaving no shadowy corners. Adjustable track lights can provide either ambient or task lighting, and they can be repositioned easily if the room is reorganized.

Nonglare task lighting should evenly illuminate the entire work or play area. For full coverage, ceiling lights for a desk should be as far behind as the desk is long—18 in. behind an 18-in. desk, for instance. Reading lights should beam over the reader's shoulder.

Don't forget natural light. If windows are skimpy or absent, consider adding a skylight.

▲ KIDS LOVE RUSTIC ROOMS with their promise of imaginary escape to someplace wild and adventurous. Hefty log beds, plank flooring, and paneled walls give this rugged room the allure of a house in the woods. Tucking the upper bunk against a low ceiling makes it safe as well as cozy.

◄ THE CANVAS-COVERED CEILING and raw wood molding turn a bedroom into safari digs. The fake ventilation hole, complete with faux fern, and the swinging seat add to the atmosphere—and the fun. Animal-print accessories complete the look and can be easily replaced as the child grows.

▲ EVERYTHING IS WOOD—or looks like it—in this easy-to-assemble camping room. Log wallpaper runs up to the plate shelf, which functions as a window ledge, display surface, and visual cap for the cabin space. Perching the bunkhouse bed on high crossbars makes the room feel big and open.

◄ THIS CABIN ROOM, with walls of rough-sawn plywood panels and a no-frills plywood closet, looks and lives like camp. The beds were made with real trees salvaged from construction sites. For a cozy touch, each bed has its own window and reading light.

COOL ILLUSIONS

▲ FANTASY HAS NO BOUNDS when illusion and reality merge. The gargoyle and overhead shelf fit perfectly into the painted castle wall. Rope lighting gives the shelf a dreamy glow, and small spotlights inset in the shelf bring each faux scene to life.

▶ A VERITABLE DREAM MACHINE, this room features a bed platform in the shape of a draw-bridge, which extends down from the painted castle wall. The friendly dragon, cheerful court jester, and knight in shining armor ensure a safe and pleasant sleep.

▶ SPECIAL EFFECTS open this room to the night sky. Glow-in-the-dark wallpaper runs across the ceiling and down the top foot of the walls, capping the room in stars. The faux window opens to a dramatic, looming moon. Real molding over the window intensifies the illusion while adding display space.

▲ YOU CAN ALMOST HEAR the dinosaurs roar in this wild scene. Each Masonite® behemoth is glued to a wood block so it pops right out of the landscape.

CREATIVE USE OF SPACE

▶ AROUND THE ROOM, built-in drawers, shelves, and a desktop (not shown) punctuate the wainscoting, furnishing the space without intruding on floor area. A low opening leads to a hideout that occupies surplus knee-wall space.

▼ TUCKED AGAINST THE WALL, this furniture-quality platform loft yields bonus play area over the bed and a snug shelter around it. The side columns accommodate deep shelves, and each step houses a drawer. Even the footboard is a container: One hollow post is a secret compartment, and the other holds a time capsule.

▲ ▶ THE YOUNG *STAR WARS* FAN doesn't yet need a walk-in closet, so for now his is a play annex. The metallic paint glaze promotes a sci-fi look, while foam-backed commercial carpeting makes a durable yet forgiving surface that's firm enough for rolling toys. In the bedroom, the top-only bunk bed leaves space for a seating alcove.

▼ THE HOUSE MOTIF unifies the structures in this room, and their placement and orientation organizes the space. The red-roofed, side-facing unit defines the computer center on one side, while the blue, front-facing case keeps books accessible to the desk on the other.

▲ DON'T RULE OUT THE ATTIC as bedroom territory just because the space is irregular. Sheathed in beadboard panels that contrast with surrounding walls, the chimney cone is the star of this room. Windows add light to expand the usable space; placed low to fit into the wall, they should open only partway to ensure safety.

► SHELVES CAPTURE otherwise under-used space in the closet, keeping toys organized. With stacked rods, the closet offers plenty of accessible clothing storage for now and in the future when the child is older, taller, and has a wider range of attire.

▼ ON THE OTHER SIDE of the room a quilted fabric panel presses the wall into service as a display board over the built-in desk. The panel blends in with the funky laminate that coordinates the drawers and countertops.

SLEEPY-TIME NOOKS

▶ THIS SOFTLY LIGHTED NOOK encloses only half the bed, but that's enough to form a cozy bed niche. A poster-width wall and recessed bookshelves personalize the space. The other half of the bed doubles as a couch with bolster "arms" and built-in side tables.

◀ THE SLEEP ALCOVE and walk-in closet share a wall, tucking away both bed and belongings to leave plenty of play space. The alcove stands out as a unit, though, with its brilliant, contrasting color and wide molding at top and bottom. Inside, a reading light has pale pink glass for atmosphere.

▲ THE DRYWALL ARCHWAY forms an enchanting, skylighted niche for a child—and all her favorite toys. For visual balance, the recessed wall and stock, quarter-round windows echo the archway shape. Brackets hold the mattress in place and ease the job of bed making. There's a trundle bed underneath for guests.

◄ SOFT COLORS, a deeply angled opening, and the glow of an interior light accentuate the comfort and coziness of this bed cove. Fitted with private shelves, the niche is an exclusive retreat that preserves floor area, and the trundle bed can be rolled out for sleepovers.

BEDS MADE EASY

► WITH A FEW STRINGS ATTACHED, you can turn a canopy bed into a dreamy hideaway. Give it tentlike height by adding a peak or two using monofilament fishing line tacked or hooked to the ceiling. Monofilament makes a "rod" for the curtains, too.

▲ EVEN IF SPACE IS TOO TIGHT for a conventional headboard, there's room for a board like this. It was cut from Masonite, then painted and affixed to the wall with a couple of nails. The Masonite "bedside lamp" is a whimsical touch.

Making Cool Kids' Furniture

CREATING AN IMAGINATIVE BED, playhouse, or other structure for your child's room need not be daunting. Step-by-step design guides and primers on constructing wood furniture are available on the Internet and at your library. To make it even easier, an array of plans, kits, and unfinished furniture is available for purchase, as are tips and aids for decorating the furniture.

Many companies offer choices of colors and features for their kids' furniture, and some will customize products to match your needs. This bed loft/bookcase combo is an example of the products available from an Internet-based retailer. It can be ordered as a plan or as a kit of ready-to-assemble parts, either unpainted, primed, or fully painted.

► DESIGNED TO FIT OVER A TWIN BED, this loft arrives as a package of components to be screwed together. It comes unfinished or painted in various motifs. If you are good with tools, you can buy just the plan and build the loft yourself.

A BED MADE BETTER

An inexpensive pine bunk bed can easily be morphed into an adventure center. For strength and stability, a sheet of veneer plywood is screwed to the back of this structure. Another plywood sheet turns the upper bunk into a play platform with hinged trapdoors.

The smaller trapdoor just fits a rope-hung bucket, which can fish up messages or toys.

The hinged trapdoor opens upward, making way for a child to crawl through.

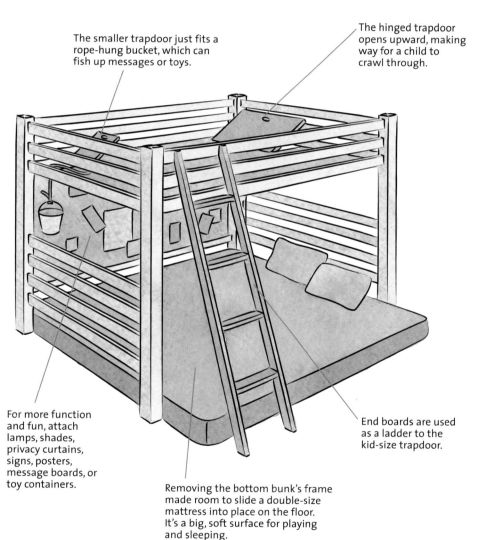

For more function and fun, attach lamps, shades, privacy curtains, signs, posters, message boards, or toy containers.

End boards are used as a ladder to the kid-size trapdoor.

Removing the bottom bunk's frame made room to slide a double-size mattress into place on the floor. It's a big, soft surface for playing and sleeping.

▲ WITH AN UPPER BUNK/PLAY SPACE, a trundle bed, and plenty of open floor area, this masculine room is ready for a crowd of little boys. The beds are crafted from rough-hewn pine logs, while draperies hang on fishing poles. The rug was made with inexpensive carpet pieced together on site.

▶ THIS LOFT takes the playhouse idea to a new level, as it creates the illusion of a shingled house-within-a-house. It's a 5-ft. by 12-ft. room that fills surplus attic space. The glassless window openings soak in light from the skylight. The loft is carpeted and has a fiberboard wall where pictures can be tacked up.

▲ THE LOWER BUNK is a cozy haven that offers a full-size bed. But when friends come to play, everybody heads up the ladder to the "second floor," which has both a twin-size mattress under the roof and a railed passageway. The outside wall of the structure is lined with bookshelves for smart storage.

▲ TO MATCH THE PLASTER WALLS, this new closet was framed in and built using blueboard with a plaster skin coat. The doors are glass-paneled units ordered without the glass, then backed with fabric. When the room décor changes, the fabric can be changed, too. The classic built-in study unit also can be adapted as the child grows—the shelves are adjustable, and the green knobs can be replaced easily.

▲ THESE FURNITURE-QUALITY built-in cabinets give shape to the room and create a niche for the bed. The top shelves are designed for display. The others are adjustable—and removable—to hold books and toys of different sizes.

◄ WALLS TOO NARROW FOR FURNITURE can be put to use with built-in shelving. This tall unit on a sliver of wall between a window and closet houses a cabinet plus adjustable shelves. It's balanced by a matching unit on the other side of the window; the two built-ins frame the opening for the window seat.

▲ ▶ CONCEAL CD PLAYERS and television sets in enclosures that add style to the room. The "dollhouse" adorning the dresser is actually a television cabinet that's constructed of plywood and pierced with holes in the back for wiring.

ADDED DIMENSIONS

▲ THE THREE-DIMENSIONAL OBJECTS hanging on branches make this painted tree seem more real while also providing ingenious display space. The birdhouse shelf is on picture hangers; the clothesline is nailed into place.

▼ BOXED OUT just a few inches from the wall, this headboard doubles as a puppet stage. For kids with other interests, such an opening could be used for dangling fish, planets, butterflies, or airplanes.

The Real Thing

BRING NOVEL FEATURES into your child's room to create an environment where fantasies become reality—well, almost. Here are some possibilities that may enchant your child.

- Budding dancers will take great pleasure in performing at a ballet barre affixed to a mirrored wall.
- Golf aficionados can putter around at a carpeted corner mound that works like a green.
- For rising music stars, build a small stage equipped with a basic home karaoke system.
- Wannabe firefighters can stimulate their imaginations—and burn off some excess energy—by sliding down their own fire pole. Build a ladder on a nearby wall for access to the pole top.
- Kids love horses. Install a carousel-style horse that children can cherish for its beauty and ride for the fun.

▶ THIS FIRE POLE is bolted securely at the top and bottom and is surrounded with carpeting for a soft landing.

Perfect for Preteens

PRETEENS WANT TO EXPRESS who they are, but they also want to be like their friends. The result is a room that should make two statements: This is me, and I'm cool. Girls may prefer brassy rooms showcasing pop stars, or they may opt for flowery, feminine spaces. Boys may go for extreme themes, featuring sports, outer space, or science-fiction characters. In terms of storage, preteens, especially girls, will be able to fill jumbo drawers and expansive closets with clothes.

Many kids have also amassed quite a collection of memorabilia from events and activities by this age. These things merit prominent display around the room because they demonstrate defining accomplishments and experiences that lend a constant source of encouragement. A comfy corner designated for the computer—whether for work or play—is a smart addition, as is a snug bed niche where kids can be alone with their thoughts—or their headphones.

▼ FRILLS AND FEMININE COLORS are the sugar and funky details are the spice. Painted accents and playful curves in the facing make the hutch and under-window storage units cool for kids. So do the headboard and footboard, which are inverse pieces cut from the same board.

▲ DIVIDING THIS ROOM into sections organizes the space while adding personality. The sunny dormers have been turned into curtained hideaways or reading nooks. The blue ceiling defines the bedroom area and gives it a soft, feminine aura. At the other end of the room (not shown) there is a sitting area along with a computer corner.

◄ THE SINGLE-MINDEDNESS of this basketball room is a slam dunk for a preteen boy, as is the hands-on, shoot-the-hoops basket in the corner. The dashes and half balls on the wall are an inexpensive and easy-to-produce standing invitation to play.

CREATING ATMOSPHERE

▲ THIS COLORFUL BUILT-IN has the interest and diversity of a room full of furniture. The three sections—six-drawer bureau (not shown), central desk, and toy cabinet— have adjustable shelves on top. Green backing unifies the unit, while vertical dividers and facings add zest.

◄ A SLOPED CEILING can be used as a natural overhang, eliminating the need for canopy bed-posts. Even more cool, the bed's side curtain can be unhooked to enclose a private retreat. Bump up the ceiling, and the dormer window becomes a bright, inviting study niche.

◄ GIRLS LOVE "SKY ROOMS" with blue heavens and puffy clouds. This one has extra appeal because the painted sky continues across the blinds. Rope lighting highlights this hip feature.

▼ PRETEENS CAN JAZZ UP a bedroom wall all on their own by using simple knickknack shelves, a dash of paint, and a creative arrangement of stick-on wallpaper accents.

CAPTURING EXTRA SPACE

▲ ACTIVITY SPACE under a loft bed is as popular with preteens as it is with younger children, but instead of toy shelves and a play table, the preteens make use of it for clothing storage and a desk. Pulling the structure away from the wall makes room for a bureau and wall-hung shelves.

◄ ▼ THIS EFFICIENT STRUCTURE corrects the deficiencies of a small, closetless room, carving out space for a full-size bunk, a locker-look closet, and a sitting nook. On the opposite wall, corner shelves capture display space alongside the built-in cabinetry.

▶ **BUILT-INS CONTRIBUTE INTEREST** and capacity to a bland, rectangular room. The window seat and shelving wrap around this sunny corner, taking up little room but adding considerable storage. They also define an inviting reading and relaxation zone.

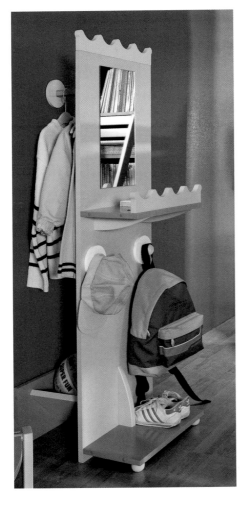

◀ A TWO-SIDED STORAGE PIER doubles the storage potential while taking up only a few more inches of space than conventional shelving. Equipped with a mirror and shelf, this one even works as a dresser.

▶ TWO STANDARD CLOSETS may help keep things more organized than one large one. Another big advantage is that they form a niche for a dresser with walls on three sides for mirrors and bulletin boards. Provide lighting overhead or above the mirror.

Powering Up

AS KIDS GROW UP, so do their electrical needs. They steadily accumulate electronic equipment, from computers and phones to audio systems, DVD players, accent lights, hair irons—you name it. Plan ahead for this surge of power usage by installing ample wiring and outlets.

Circle the room with outlets placed no more than 12 ft. apart so there's always one nearby. Run a high-capacity, CAT-5 cable to the desk area and provide at least two duplex receptacles there for the computer, monitor, and desk lamp. Install a phone jack at the desk and at least one more elsewhere in the room.

A three-way switch to the bedside lamp gives both you and your child the option of turning the light on or off at the nightstand or at the door.

◀ THIS CABINET WALL, which organized the space when it was a nursery and then a toddler's room, still does the job for the preteen who now inhabits it, holding all of her abundant belongings. Keep a few sections open for display shelves and a dressing table.

CREATIVE STANDOUTS

▼ PRETEEN BOYS like rooms that evoke adventure. This one builds on a Tom Sawyer theme, with a whitewashed fence that was apparently deserted when he was lured away by a trip to the fishing hole. The magical touch is the corner where the bed tucks inside a rail-framed cabin. The no-frills, built-in desk also has boy appeal.

▲ FINDING ADEQUATE STORAGE space is an increasing challenge as kids become more interested in clothes and accumulate other stuff. A closed unit like this wardrobe adds storage capacity without making the room too busy. In fact, the decoration makes the cabinet an important theme-setter.

Cheap Chic

CLEVER DESIGN FEATURES like those used in the room shown here are a hit with preteens and teens. Why? Because they need not cost much, they allow personal expression, and they can be accomplished by the kids themselves.

- Scour yard sales, flea markets, and secondhand stores for chairs, chests, trunks, and other furniture finds to renovate with daring paint colors and cool hardware.
- Transform old multipane windows or funky picture frames into wall mirrors by replacing the clear panes with mirror glass. Likewise, old patio doors can be re-used as closet doors, with mirrors on one side and photos, artwork, wallpaper, or paint on the other.
- Use deep-profile molding strips as shelves. Placed high on the wall, they hold decorative displays; lower shelves lend space for photos, books, and CDs. Make a fabric collage for a headboard or bulletin board. It might be a mélange of pieces from worn-out jeans or a patchwork of old team shorts and shirts.
- Shape a seating area or study by running a dowel between walls and hanging fabric from it.

▲ A STRIP OF DEEP ARCHITECTURAL MOLDING capitalizes on display space over the closet.

SPORTS STARS

► THIS RACE-CAR ROOM IS EXCITING and unusual, but it still has all the basics of a practical bedroom. Placed at a racy angle, the bed looks like the lead car rounding the track. The TV cabinet, finished with wheels and glossy auto paint, mimics a tool chest; gearshift knobs are a cool extra.

▼ GIRLS' ROOMS can be just as sporty as boys' rooms. White finishes make this room feminine while evoking the wintry scene where a snowboarder does her thing. The headboard wall is curved in a half pipe, and the shelving is designed as a chairlift ready to roll across the rope.

▼ OPPORTUNITIES TO CELEBRATE sports can be found on almost any surface of a kid's room. This dresser for a hockey fan turns pucks and a segmented stick into drawer pulls. The goal on the dresser top is made with mesh and wire.

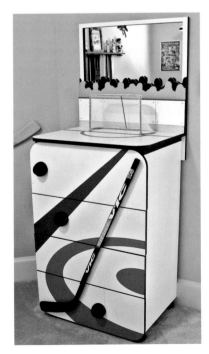

▼ THE RAISED CEILING made it possible to fulfill a basketball lover's wish to shoot hoops in his room. An extra layer of felt batts soundproofs the wood floor. The under-hoop cabinet houses the TV and sound system, while rickrack shelves display autographed balls and function as a headboard.

GARDEN VARIETIES

▼ ▶ A GARDEN ROOM makes a cheerful environment for kids of any age but is especially attractive to preteens because of its softness and femininity. Vinyl or painted wood lattice, generally available in 2-ft. by 8-ft. and 4-ft. by 8-ft. sheets, can be used to build decorative bedposts or frame a sheltered reading corner.

◄ BOLD FLOWERS, vibrant colors, and cool materials combine to produce groovy digs with flower power. The window cornices are made of pink vinyl—a hip alternative to more traditional materials such as wood. Big flowers—some dimensional, some painted—are scattered around to give the room energy and personality.

► INSTALLED A FEW INCHES FROM THE WALL, a trellis with soft arches unifies the built-ins and forms a bed niche. Mirrors in the dresser and vanity sections visually deepen the space and brighten the room with reflected light.

▲ ◄ SLIPPING A BED ALCOVE behind stands of real birch trees gives this bedroom an enchanted forest feel. The alcove provides extra storage and display space with cubicle shelving and drawers at both ends for special belongings. Fabric draped across three rods forms a canopy, and the privacy curtains have grommet holes for durability.

▼ THE LOW, ANGLED CEILING suggests a niche; the overhead light fixture, shelves, and gently molded sideboard complete it. Though shallow, the alcove is enough to make the bed corner feel cozy and private.

▲ ▼ NIFTY NICHES are dramatized to highlight the best features of this idiosyncratic room. Dressed in bright plaid, the coves and overhangs stand out especially well because every other surface recedes with a uniform coat of leafy green.

Designed and Built by Kids

WHEN CHILDREN HELP PLAN AND IMPLEMENT their room design, they create more than a room. They build pride, identity, and a healthy sense of ownership of their unique space. Along the way, they may even learn a few life lessons.

A 10-year-old girl responded enthusiastically when invited to participate in building, furnishing, and decorating her room with loft sleeping space in the family's new house. Her parents gave her a limited budget, construction help, and advice as needed, but the decisions were her own.

She collected paint samples, opting for multiple colors inspired by her duvet cover, and the family painted the room together. She developed design ideas for a headboard and furniture, which her parents helped sketch out. After buying two stools at a yard sale, she decorated them and designed a companion table, and she even cut the pieces, assembled them, and painted the table, doing the work when her father was on hand to supervise. The lessons stuck with her, and she redesigned her room again as a teen—doing the majority of the work herself!

▶ THE EXUBERANT SPIRIT OF THE PRETEEN comes through in her loft bedroom. She covered the walls and ceiling with glowing colors, built a nightstand with dowel legs, and made the sunny particleboard headboard nailed to the bed.

▼ TWO SECONDHAND STOOLS fit the preteen's low decorating budget. She pepped them up with a rainbow paint job and tacked-on canvas seat covers that she embellished with painted swirls. A homemade corner table completes the set.

▲ FOR THIS 10-YEAR-OLD, painting every surface a different, bright color felt just right. Other personal statements include the ornamental bug she made from scraps found under her father's workbench and a message mailbox on the stairs to her sleeping loft.

Teen Domains

TEENS NEED INDEPENDENCE, and they need a place where they can assert their individuality. When planning their rooms, try to give them both. Remember: Outrageous decorating is harmless.

The more self-sufficient the room, the more a teen will like it. Choose a room location that's outside the hub of family activity. If a private bathroom is not possible, consider installing a sink and vanity in the bedroom.

Help the teen design and build a bed platform, reading nook, or other cool get-away zone. Elsewhere in the room, set up a lounge (equipped with an audio-video system, a phone, and comfortable seating) where the teen can relax with friends.

Include a homework center that has ample desktop, storage, and wiring capacity. In the closet, install shelves, deep drawers, and laundry bins; if the teen decides to use them, they'll be ready and waiting.

◄ TEENS ARE READY for big, daring ideas. A step up from car-themed rooms for younger boys, this one features a bed in a steel frame supported by heavy-duty tires and chains. The realistic computer-printed mural is a more sophisticated version of the hand-painted themes you'd expect in a boy's room.

◀ THIS ROOM is almost like an apartment, perfect for independence-seeking teens. There's a "living room" seating platform for friends, a "bedroom" with both niche and loft for sleeping or reading, a study space, and lots of shelves.

▲ AN ALL-IN-ONE structure makes even a small room—in fact, especially a small room—a big hit with teens. With a queen-size bed on top, this maple unit has the dimensions to accommodate a comfortable study cubicle, two banks of dresser drawers, and deep shelves.

WONDER WALL

Add jazz to a teen's room by cutting into the wall to create a cushioned alcove.

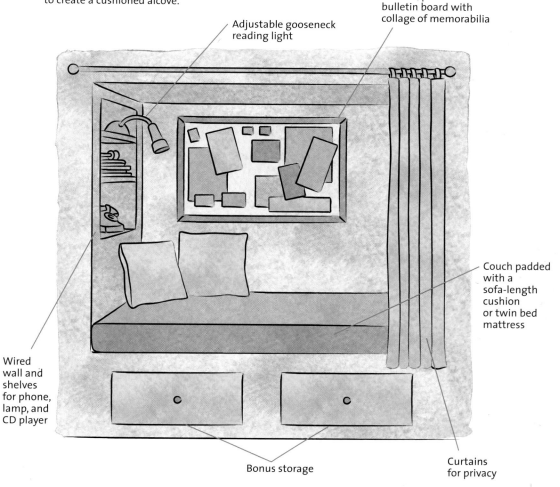

Adjustable gooseneck reading light

Framed, painted bulletin board with collage of memorabilia

Couch padded with a sofa-length cushion or twin bed mattress

Wired wall and shelves for phone, lamp, and CD player

Bonus storage

Curtains for privacy

10 Cool Ideas for Teen Rooms

THESE DIGS ARE FULL OF GOOD IDEAS, most of them generated by the teen who lives here. The room is a healthy blend of the practical and the way-out individuality most teenagers thrive on.

- The room has a separate, well-lighted study that is marked off by a short wall.
- A teen's room needs at least one show-stopping element. Here, it is the see-through fish tank on the other short wall of the study.
- The private bathroom has an extra-long counter for grooming gear.
- There's more primping space—a dressing table and a large closet with mirrored doors—outside the bathroom.
- The teen can stretch out and daydream on the long window seat. Drawers underneath hold lots of sweaters, sweatshirts, and jeans.
- She also can catch rays on her private balcony.
- Solid-core doors, carpeting, and insulated walls let her turn up the music as much as she wants.
- Parallel trim boards—at the height of the windowsill and the top of the door—hold a changing display of posters.
- Lights are on dimmer switches so they can be lowered for relaxing and listening to music.
- A curtain rod over the headboard makes it easy to change fabrics and color schemes.

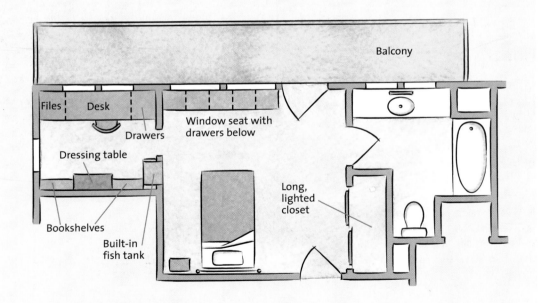

Files
Desk
Drawers
Window seat with drawers below
Dressing table
Bookshelves
Built-in fish tank
Long, lighted closet
Balcony

▲ A 6-FT. BUMPOUT over the porch adds loft space without cutting into the room's airy vaulted ceiling area. It can be used as a sleeping place for guests or a peaceful getaway.

▲ THIS TEEN'S FOUR WISHES for her space were granted: She has a loft, a reading alcove, her favorite color scheme, and not one but two big closets. All this fits into a room that is only 13 ft. by 15 ft. The book nook, at 4 ft. by 5 ft., is big enough for a comfortable chair and two bookcases suspended from the molding.

▲ FOR A TEEN who wants her own space, nothing can top a private little house—or at least a separate wing that looks like a house.

GETTING IT TOGETHER

▶ STORAGE RUNS WALL TO WALL and floor to ceiling to give this room character and make every inch count. Along with drawers and a cool collage of display shelves, this setup houses user-friendly catchall bins. When tucked under the shelving, the bed functions as a couch.

◀ THOUGH MOST TEENS tend to litter the floor with clothes, they find neater surroundings less stressful. A hamper like this conceals the mess and is so convenient that teens might actually use it; the removable bin also saves a little hassle at laundry time.

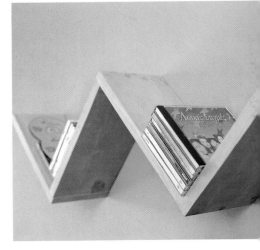

▶ CD AND DVD collections tend to stack up, like clothes, on the floor. Rickrack shelves by the computer or DVD player are a practical alternative since they keep the collections in view. They are easy to make with pine boards, some nails, and carpenter's glue.

GRADUATING TO ADULTHOOD

► A LOCKER ROOM THEME is fun for teens, but the quality materials and classy graphic treatment of these built-ins will hold their appeal for years. An acid wash makes the ash cabinetry look metallic; the painted walls are faux denim.

▼ THIS ROOM STRIKES a good balance between teen-friendly and adult-friendly; it has a few trendy touches, but the basic fixtures and colors are all timeless, muted, and sophisticated. The slim shelving and wraparound cabinetry is ample enough to house an evolving collection of items as the teenager grows up.

Shared Spaces

SOMETIMES SIBLINGS WANT TO BE TOGETHER, and sometimes they absolutely don't. A shared bedroom should respect that reality, encompassing common areas for play and conversation, and exclusive territory for each child to sleep, study, or simply get away.

Use furniture arrangements or low partitions to mark the boundaries between common and private zones. Shared territory may include an open area for active play, plus stations for games, crafts, and other activities involving communal toys.

Private zones should be designed to create a sense of separation from the center of activity. Strive for equity rather than sameness with these individual areas. Equip each with separate lighting, storage compartments, and display space for favorite things.

Coming up with a design motif that satisfies everyone calls for flexibility. With your kids' input, choose a family of colors, patterns, and furniture styles. Then use them to express both togetherness and each child's individuality.

◀ SMALL, SHARED ROOMS may not offer the luxury of completely separate territory for each child. This room solves the problem by radiating the built-in beds in different directions, giving each child a sense of privacy—and his own window.

▶ THE BOUNDARIES defining private and shared spaces are friendly but clear here. The open framework between loft beds encloses a communal window-side play center and also marks the boundary of each child's corner. Like little rooms, the corners include bed, drawers, shelving, and display space. The loft areas are separate but linked for versatility.

▲ THIS ROOM HAS A GOOD MIX of open play space, areas for group or individual activities, snug bed enclosures, and guest beds. Wainscoting, rails, and the overhanging loft enfold the beds in cozy niches, with trundles beneath. The loft works as a play area or third guest bed.

◄ THE FLOOR-TO-CEILING FOOTBOARDS on these beds function as partitions between sleeping and activity space. On one side, they shape cozy bed enclosures. On the other, they form walls for built-in desks with overhead lighting that won't disturb the kids who have turned in for the night.

TOGETHERNESS FOR FUN

▶ THE RAISED FLOOR and framework of overhead soffit and slim castle towers make this shared play space an enchanting destination. They also mark a useful boundary between play area and sleeping area, doing so without blocking the window.

▼ INSTEAD OF SMALLER, separate bedrooms, space was allocated in this house to give the kids one larger, shared room. The plan nets a big activity table and an indoor playground, complete with swing. Each child still has a private bed nook with drawers and display walls.

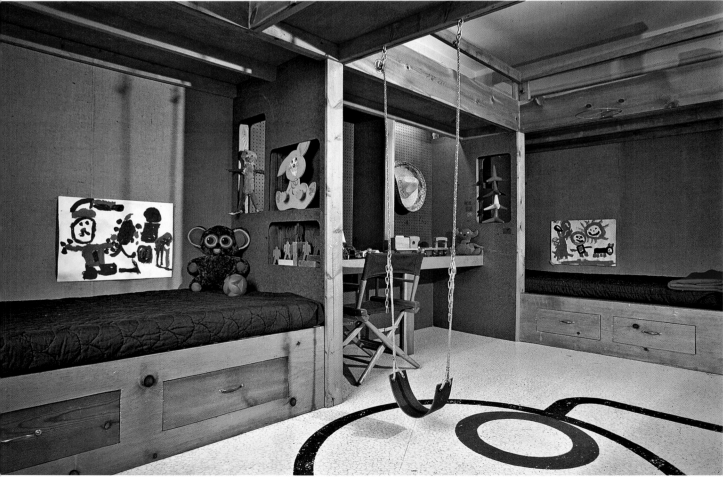

◄ ▲ WHEN THEY FEEL like hanging out together, the boys can shoot hoops at one end of their room or watch a video at the other. When they want some personal space, they have it—in study niches and bed alcoves.

SMALL SPACE, BIG IDEAS

▲ THIS EFFICIENT ROOM packs in lots of utility while preserving open play space and a bright, uncluttered look. The white closets blend into the background with fabric-lined doors that look like wall panels. For comfort and space conservation, the bunks have padded, wall-mounted "headboards." The bunk stairs contain drawers.

▲ ▼ MURPHY BEDS and a fold-down table enable this room to do double duty. At night it comfortably accommodates two beds and a shared game table. When the beds and table fold away during the day, the room becomes a play area with a decorative paneled wall.

SPECIAL CONNECTIONS

◄ WHEN SIBLINGS have adjacent rooms, there's an opportunity for playful connections. The half door that separates these sisters' rooms lends an air of intrigue while providing privacy when needed. It can be replaced with drywall or shelving if it proves to be too much togetherness when they get older.

CLOSET CONNECTION

Linking rooms with a closet corridor offers many advantages. Young children can use one room in the suite as a playroom and the other as a shared bedroom. Later they get separate, connecting bedrooms, with the option of closing the mirrored closet doors for privacy or quiet.

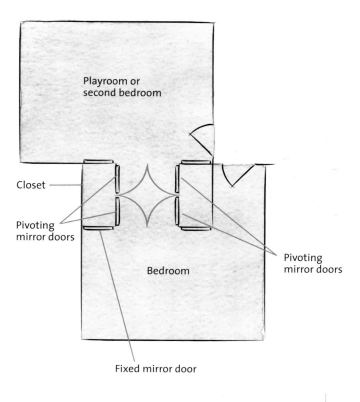

Playroom or second bedroom

Closet

Pivoting mirror doors

Pivoting mirror doors

Bedroom

Fixed mirror door

▶ A BROTHER AND SISTER can exchange toys or messages using this little pass-through in the wall between their rooms. There's a 6-in. by 10-in. door at each end, and each child has a skeleton key to lock the door for privacy.

SWEET SUITES

▲ EFFECTIVE ZONING turns this attic room into a versatile suite for two children. The broad, lighted window bay houses a two-person homework area, an inviting window seat with bench storage, and open shelving sized to hold see-through plastic containers for toys and computer games.

◄ THE FAUX FIREPLACE is a fun device for defining the sitting area. Recessed built-ins stow books, clothing, the television, and the audio system. With easy access to the wall from adjacent attic space, these shelves can easily be wired for conversion to a media center.

10 Cool Ideas for Kids' Suites

MULTIROOM SUITES give siblings the best of two worlds—bedrooms of their own plus common ground for play and study. Two sisters share this suite, an attic conversion that's filled with good ideas.

- The bedrooms are well separated by the shared space.
- The common area occupies an extended hall at the top of the stairs. It makes dynamic use of the space and keeps the kids' area separate but not isolated from the family area downstairs.
- Drywall partitions give each bedroom its own cool character. Walls in one room enclose a deep and dreamy bed niche.

- Partitions in the other bedroom frame a sitting nook and walk-in closets.
- The shared space is organized into zones for playing, watching TV, and studying.
- A dormer was made into a little room. The girls use it as a hideout. For sleepovers, it's the perfect place to spread out sleeping bags.
- No space is wasted. Shelves lining a narrow wall between rooms make a handy game garage.
- There's only one bathroom, but it includes a sink for each child.
- The kids have their own laundry area.
- Closets fill spare corners, giving each child storage space for her own stuff.

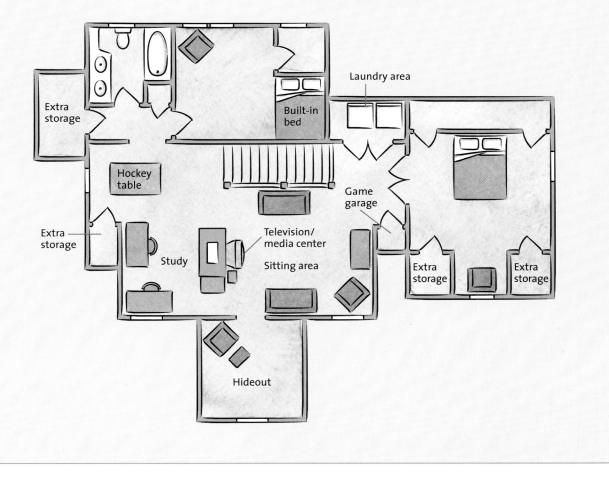

Extra storage

Built-in bed

Laundry area

Hockey table

Extra storage

Study

Television/ media center

Sitting area

Game garage

Extra storage

Extra storage

Hideout

PERSONAL TURF

▼ ► **THESE COZY BED FORTS** face each other so the kids can talk, but they're otherwise private and self-sufficient. Each contains a tabletop/deep display shelf under the eaves, under-bed drawers, a closet at one end, and a desk and bookshelves in the sitting area at the other. The children can keep a lookout through the portholes.

◄ ▼ DOUBLE-SIZE BUNK BEDS make private retreats with elbow room and enough space for a friend to sleep over. The bunks are complementary but unique, with curtains and a ladder on one, and rails and whimsical jack-and-the-beanstalk steps on the other. The three-quarter-height chair rail opens up wall space for cheery vertical stripes.

SEPARATION BY DESIGN

▼ THE CRENELLATED BUILT-IN between these beds enhances the room's castle theme and has several practical advantages, too. Most important, it separates the beds, giving each child some privacy. Also, the open shelves provide display and storage space without blocking light from the window.

► THIS DEEP, WIDE DORMER is just right for a toddler's bed. The toddler gets a special little nook, and one that steals no general floor space from the shared room. When she outgrows the nook, a window seat can be built there.

▼ COLOR-CODING gives this room a coordinated look while making each child's space unique. A trim piece across the top makes each bed niche feel a little more sheltered and private. Each niche has its own inset shelf, too.

Rooms That Grow Up

A ROOM THAT'S IDEAL for a child today will need to change eventually, as the child gets bigger, develops different interests, and accumulates belongings. By thinking ahead, you can ease the rearrangement process and avoid expensive redos.

Focus on shaping a room that can evolve, constructing a play platform that could morph into a teenager's lounge, for instance, or building an extra closet that will work as a clubhouse, bed loft, or study alcove.

Invest in adaptable furnishings that will hold up to years of use. Choose adjustable shelving, closet rods, and desk chairs. Classic, modular storage and countertop systems are great because they can be shuffled or supplemented as needed. Depending on the setup, they can form play stations or homework centers, strips of toy bins or stacked units that divide the room into sections.

Let your kids add the accent colors, patterns, and accessories of the moment. When the times change, these confections can easily be changed, too.

▲ THIS WALL UNIT keeps pace with a child's needs, from infancy on. The changing table and rolling toy box come out to reveal a pre-finished desk. The cabinet, with drawers and adjustable shelves and rods, can hold baby supplies, toys, books, clothes, or a television and other equipment.

▶ THIS ROOM WAS DESIGNED TO PLEASE a toddler and work for a boy as a preteen through young adult. The toddler's bed structure is whimsical and colorful, with a fanciful townscape headboard, toy drawers featuring geometric shapes, and a picture-book-size bookshelf. The bedside stepstool is also a toy box.

► A SPORTS THEME replaced the toddler motif when the boy became a preteen. The bed was painted blue, and the footboard and window cornice board were covered with padded, football-colored vinyl. Refinished, the drawers now look like vintage suitcases. Banquette-style panels frame a headboard corner for reading or watching TV.

◄ TO SCORE MORE POINTS with the preteen, a dresser on the opposite wall was replaced by a built-in desk and cabinetry finished in sporty natural wood and pigskin-colored vinyl that matches the bed. The curtain tiebacks are real leather—made from retooled old belts.

AGES AND STAGES

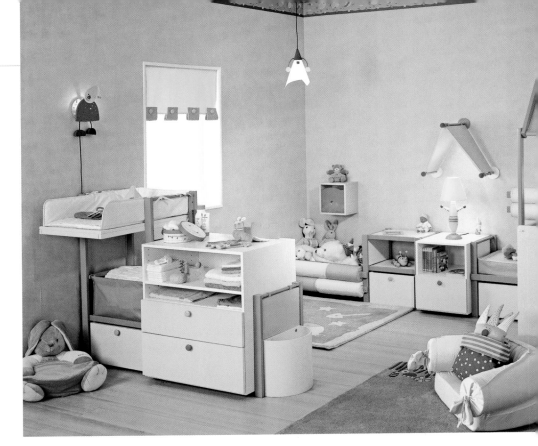

▶ AN EXPANDING SUITE of adaptable components enables this room to grow with the child. As a nursery, it clusters supply storage and diaper bin with the changing table. Toys are in low containers where a baby can look at them and a beginning walker can reach them. A roof over the crib, and another over the lamp, add whimsy.

▶ HEIGHTENED ADVENTURE suits a grade school child. Raised on posts, the railed bed becomes a loft and fort, complete with reused lamp roof. Toy storage and a curtained reading corner/guest bed fit underneath, and hobby shelves have been added to the storage mix. The lighted desk is ready for play or homework.

◄ FOR A TODDLER a low, railed bed replaces the crib, but the cozy roof canopy remains. Lowered, the changing table has become a play table. The diaper bin now holds toys. More cabinets, some taller, contain the toddler's growing inventory of toys, books, and clothes.

◄ FOR A PRETEEN or teen, the room has a fully equipped homework alcove under a taller bed loft. Tucked under the bookshelf, the guest bed doubles as seating. Open shelving can hold a variety of things—sound system, CDs, television, books. Bins keep clothes and sports gear off the floor.

STORAGE TRANSFORMED

▼ ▶ THE BASIC ORGANIZATION of this closet system—columns of rods, shelves, and sliders—accommodates the changing needs of kids from infancy through the teen years. That's because the components are adjustable, removable, and replaceable. Young children like low bins, while preteens and teens need more drawers and shelves.

FABRIC COVERING turns an economical coated-steel unit into versatile, fun storage. In the nursery, a tent features closeable flaps that hide clutter and handy side pockets for small toys and essentials. For a toddler, the storage unit becomes a toy shelf with a playful cloth cover that's open for easy access and sports oversize side pockets.

Splashy Bathrooms

Personality is what makes kids' bathrooms great, but they need to be hardworking, too. To make the most of this small room with so many functional requirements, start by analyzing how your kids will use the space. Kids are more likely to put away their towels and shampoo if hooks and shelves are both plentiful and conveniently located. Place lighting so that it will effectively illuminate the sink, bath or shower, and dressing area. Small children need a boost to reach a standard-height sink; either lower part of the vanity or include a step stool. It's also smart to provide ample separation between the tub/shower and vanity areas so your kids can share the bathroom without getting in each other's way.

Outfitting a bathroom to indulge your kids' sense of fun is easier than ever. Manufacturers are offering an increasingly wide range of accent tiles, laminates, wall coverings, faucet handles, drawer pulls, and bath accessories that fit kids' themes. Choose lively highlights, but opt for fixtures, vanities, flooring, and general wall tile that will age well. With a good, basic room arrangement in place, it will be simple to update the bath as your children get older.

◄ PLAYFUL POINTS OF COLOR make this otherwise grown-up bathroom youthful and fresh. A whimsical paint job inexpensively transforms the old tub into a design highlight; a shower-curtain ring can be added later. Custom sea-theme floor and wall tiles fit into the grid of commercial tiles.

Extreme Themes

DO YOUR KIDS HAVE A CONSUMING INTEREST in pirates, mermaids, or jungle animals? If so, go for it. Drench the bathroom in that theme, bearing in mind that the room will need an update sooner than one designed with less gusto. Stick with a neutral tub, shower, sink, and toilet, as these can be made to blend into almost any design. Beyond that, the whole room is your canvas.

A theme can be expressed with color, pattern, and/or texture, along with retail or custom-made accessories, from drawer pulls to decorative tiles to fantastical built-in units. Keep in mind, though, that a small bathroom can be overwhelmed with a complex design scheme. The more components you include, the simpler they should be.

▲ WHITEWASHED WOOD, a sky-blue wall, and green tile evoke a garden with a rustic picket fence, but the sponge-painted drywall clouds take the outdoor theme over the top. The clouds also serve a functional purpose by concealing can lights. Staggering the vanity height customizes the sinks for each child.

▲ THIS INDOOR "OUTHOUSE" was simple enough to construct around a regular toilet, but it lends a big sense of wit to an otherwise traditional boy's bathroom. Tucked against the wall, the private compartment is ventilated on all sides and has an overhead light. A clubhouse like this would make a great closet, too.

▲ LARGE-FORMAT WALLPAPER borders and murals create the illusion of being on board a ship. The baseboard and paneled tub surround enhance the effect by simulating the perspective of a ship's railing from the deck. The basics—a pedestal sink, white tub, and wood medicine cabinet—will transition well when these kids outgrow their seafaring days.

◀ TAKE THE PLUNGE with a total-surround design. Covering walls, ceiling, and countertop, this deep blue sea envelops the room, creating an animated, dramatic environment. The solid-surface vanity top has an integrated sink that seamlessly continues the flow of blue. Sand-colored cabinetry lends visual variety within the sea theme.

Accent Details

YOU DON'T HAVE TO GO WITH an all-out theme to give a kid's bath character. Spice up the room with easily changed elements such as stenciled wall decorations and fanciful door and drawer pulls. A vibrant paint job on molding, window frames, and open shelving is a simple and inexpensive way to add zip to existing architectural details. If you have a creative itch, paint the sink or tub with a few choice specimens of your kid's favorite flora or fauna to give it even more personality.

Using accent tiles—whether border strips, picture tiles, embossed pieces, or even solid color tiles in interesting shapes and placements—provides visual delight. You and your kids can even design your own tiles, making handprints, painting the tiles, or having a ceramic artist make them for you. Custom tiles can be pricey, but you won't need many.

▼ SPARE USE OF COLOR makes this bathroom sparkle, placing the focus on the room's clean lines and fresh accents. The dramatic teal vessel sink and other spots of color—drawer pulls, ceramic tile accent strips, mosaic floor tiles—create a friendly space for children that will retain its appeal even as they grow up.

▲ OTHERWISE NEUTRAL, this boy's bathroom comes alive with forest images, from the bear tiles over the tub to the painted moose and busy beaver. The atmosphere of adventure makes the room a delight, as does the camouflaged door (on the opposite wall), which connects to an adjoining room.

Styling with Tile

A GREAT WAY to make a kid's bathroom sparkle is to use decorative ceramic tiles. They're durable, they're waterproof, and they're available in hundreds of shapes, colors, sizes, motifs, and profiles for use on floors, walls, countertops, and backsplashes.

You won't need many decorative tiles to make the design complete. Choose a theme and/or a color scheme and apply it judiciously, perhaps with a few colorful, pictorial tiles and a coordinating border of linear ceramic strips. Before buying tiles, bring home several samples to try out the sizes and colors in the bathroom.

For a more personal touch, design your own tiles. You can paint images onto existing tiles using oil-based paint over a latex-based primer-sealer. There are commercial services that will transfer your favorite images—decals, photos, kids' drawings and paintings—onto new tiles. Or you can make the tiles yourself at a crafts activity store. Be sure the decorative tiles are sized to fit with the tiles that will surround them when installed.

A tile floor or wall in one brilliant color may be all you need. The floor tile should have a nonskid finish. You can even select colored grout to offset the tiles. Thin grout lines are easiest to keep clean.

▲ A RAINBOW OF TROPICAL FISH **swims** on the tiled wall, providing a focal point of color. Floor tiles in mottled ocean shades accentuate the sea theme; their small size makes the room seem bigger.

▶ A SPRINKLING OF SPRIGHTLY ANIMALS **and insects** and a ribbon of green are all that's needed to convey a fresh riverside theme. The tiles are turned so the colorful creatures hop every which way.

DETACHABLE DECOR

▼ ▶ WALLPAPER CUTOUTS **work not only on walls but also on tubs, tiles, mirrors, or any smooth surface that will not be exposed directly to high moisture. These shells and dolphins are sold pre-cut, prepasted, and ready to apply, but you can also make them from vinyl-coated, prepasted wallpaper. To remove, just wet them again.**

Do-It-Yourself Wall Designs

HUNDREDS OF PATTERNS **are available for youthful wallpaper, borders, and murals, but children take special joy in patterns they help to plan and create. It's never been easier to give wall designs that personal imprint.**

   One approach is to transfer design outlines directly onto the wall and fill them in with paint. Create the designs by drawing around puzzle pieces, cookie cutters, cutout pictures, or favorite characters traced from books. Or take your child's black-and-white line drawing to the local rubber stamp shop and have it made into a stamp to use on the wall. If you prefer ready-made stamps, let your child choose from the wide variety of whimsical art stamps available through hobby shops, rubber stamp retailers, and stamp Web sites.

   Another approach is to design custom wall covering. This used to be very pricey, but digital printing has made it affordable for small, residential projects. Once scanned for conversion to a digital image, any design—including your child's art—can be transferred onto easy-to-install vinyl wall covering that comes to you in rolls. There's an hourly charge to finalize the design and prepare it for printing; the printing cost is calculated by square foot (generally about $8 a square foot or less). The larger the quantity, the lower the rate.

◄ ROLLED IN TO DELIGHT a toddler, these cars and buses can hit the road as soon as the child's interests shift, since they are removable, reusable peel-and-stick pictures. Accessories like these are widely available and versatile, as they can be used individually, in collages, or as borders.

▼ FOR HIS BATHROOM, a little boy drew outlines of pictures that were then made into rubber stamps. Once the outlines were stamped onto the wall, he helped paint them in.

▲ THE INTERIOR DESIGNER DREW THE LIVELY LIZARD that populates this custom-printed wallpaper, but the scene could have been drawn by the brothers who share the bathroom.

Using Every Inch

EVERY INCH COUNTS in kids' bathrooms, since they usually are small. Maximize the circulation area by spacing the fixtures around the room. Shallow shelves and compact cabinets can put wall areas to productive use without absorbing much floor space. Open shelves make it easy for kids to find the things they need—and put them away. Hooks for robes and towels should be big, colorful, and low for the same reason. And as in other kids' rooms, quirky spaces, such as tight corners or low ceilings, can be used to advantage in bathrooms.

When kids share a bathroom, turf issues come into play. If there's room for only one sink, at least give each child separate storage and counter space. Install partial walls or partitions at the commode and bathing areas. These dividers afford privacy, and also create extra surfaces for inset shelves and towel bars.

▲ PARTIAL WALLS compartmentalize the room without compromising the sense of space. The yellow wall frames the shower, and the half-height tiled wall defines the vanity area while providing some privacy for the commode. A central skylight provides even light during the day and is supplemented at night by light from ceiling and vanity fixtures.

▶ THE IRREGULAR SHAPE of the bathroom gives this vanity its own well-lighted niche. There's another vanity at the other end of the room for a sibling. The tub is open at foot and side, giving parents easy access at bath time. With a handheld shower spray, it's ready to go when the kids make the transition to showers.

10 Cool Ideas for Kids' Bathrooms

- Tuck lockers between wall studs to keep each child's bathroom gear separate, organized, and out of sight. Buy metal units or make lockers out of laminated wood. Personalize them with color, graphics, or nameplates.
- Punctuate the walls with cubbies that keep towels, toys, and toothbrushes handy.
- Paint your own tiles to add zing to the walls, floor, or tub surround.
- Sprinkle big hooks or fanciful knobs around the room at heights each child can easily reach. Color-coordinate them with drawer pulls and cabinet hardware.
- Over the sink, attach a mirror that tilts down for small children to use.
- Instead of a drawer, slide a step into the base of the vanity to give kids a boost.
- Install dual sinks, one low and one standard height. Wire the spot so that later you can replace the low sink with a compact washing machine for the kids.
- Add a brightly painted accordion door that becomes a divider as needed between vanity and tub or commode.
- Position the bathroom between two kids' bedrooms, with a doorway to each. Place one sink near each bedroom—or just outside the door in the bedroom itself.
- Cover the cabinet doors, toilet seat, and hamper with material to match the shower curtain.

Lockerlike cabinets and shelves can be inserted between wall studs.

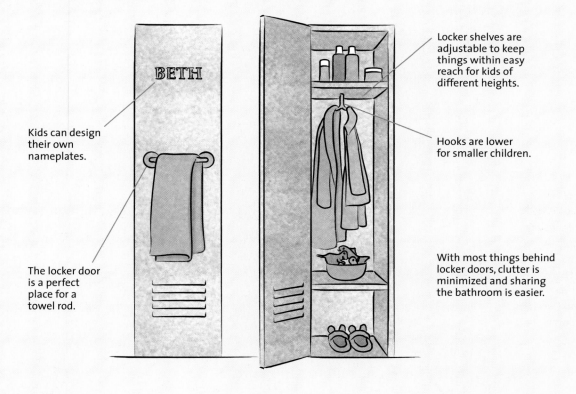

Kids can design their own nameplates.

The locker door is a perfect place for a towel rod.

Locker shelves are adjustable to keep things within easy reach for kids of different heights.

Hooks are lower for smaller children.

With most things behind locker doors, clutter is minimized and sharing the bathroom is easier.

SHARING MADE EASY

◀ ▶ A BANK OF SHELVES divides the twin-sink vanity into two distinct sections, each with its own towel bar, drawers, and cabinet. The thick middle shelf in the wall unit not only matches the countertop for visual continuity; it also clearly marks the line between each child's half of the unit. The tub/shower is on an opposite wall, as far as possible from the vanity, to separate two areas that might be used at the same time.

▼ SMART CHOICES were made about what's shared and not shared in this bathroom. To avoid skirmishes over space, each child has a sink and separate storage in the vanity. Towel rods are well spaced, too, and mounted at the right height for each child. The décor is neutral enough to be universally appealing regardless of a child's age.

Kid-Safe Bathrooms

CHILDREN'S BATHROOMS should be designed to prevent falls, burns, poisoning, and the mixing of electricity and water. Nonskid flooring is essential. So are GFCI (ground-fault circuit interrupter) outlets, which help avert shocks. Choose scald-resistant faucets or set the home water heater to no more than 120°F. Stow electrical appliances out of reach and keep medicines and toxic cleaners in locked or safety-latched cabinets.

If possible, install the sink and mirror lower than standard height so kids can use them without climbing. Otherwise, provide a sturdy stool. A stool also helps small children reach the toilet, and climb in or out of the bathtub. Grab bars in the tub or shower area are always a good idea.

BONUS SPACE

▲ COUNTER SPACE is limited in this old-style bathroom, but prefinished, molded shelves solve the problem. The ventilated radiator cover adds another countertop surface and also ensures that the kids won't burn themselves.

▲ CABINETS, SHELVES, and vanity wrap like a ribbon around the bathroom, extending countertop and storage space without encroaching on floor area in this small, attic-level room. The mirror fills the wall to capitalize on the sense of additional room created by its reflection, while the roof window adds headroom and natural light. Rounding the vanity profile expands the counter area and adds a unique touch.

◄ TO MAXIMIZE both design flexibility and floor area, this bathroom uses a pedestal sink rather than a vanity. It is supplemented by a medicine cabinet with an extra shelf, and a kid-size storage bench. The wallpaper border relieves the white walls and binds the room together. As the kids get older the room can easily be repapered and furnished with different storage units.

Grown-Up Baths

CHILDREN'S BATHROOMS DON'T HAVE TO BE CHILDISH. Sophisticated yet lighthearted designs will continue to serve your kids well from toddler to teen years, and even beyond. The key to a timeless bathroom is keeping it light, bright, and simple. Invest in full-sized fixtures in neutral shades, and high-quality faucets and lighting that will age well stylistically.

Design accents hold their freshness best when used sparingly. Select colors, contours, and motifs that have perpetual appeal—ceramic tile in rich tones or classy geometric shapes, for example. You can always add a light, youthful touch with towels, rugs, curtains, soap dishes, and other accessories that are easy to replace.

Plan ahead by building in extra drawers and cabinets to accommodate the ever-expanding array of grooming supplies your children will acquire as they grow. And they'll eventually need outlets for hair dryers, electric razors, and the like, so remember to place ample outlets around the vanity.

◄ ▲ THE UNIFYING THEME here is nothing more than circles, but they're used creatively to make the bathroom both classy and fun. Kids will like the round mirror and the funky, curved vanity with off-center sink. The frosted spheres on the very grown-up frameless glass shower door look like polka dots to the kids but are just as appealing to adults.

Freewheeling Baths

KIDS IN WHEELCHAIRS can have cool bathrooms, too. The rooms need to meet certain functional requirements, but there's no limitation on style. Widen door openings and remove thresholds, raise the toilet seat, lower the sink and cabinetry, and provide knee room and plenty of circulation space. Extend windows and mirrors downward. (Consult an accessible design specialist for the particulars.) All this can be done in the context of a great-looking bathroom. Since special attention, and possibly expense, will be devoted to selection and placement of fixtures and cabinetry, it's wise to choose a design that will endure.

The rooms shown here are good examples. Designed for a young boy, the bathroom shown at bottom right provides two bathing options—a tub and a roll-in shower with handheld spray. The half wall framing the tub makes a handy ledge to hold on to. Bands of diamond-shaped tiles are bold but not juvenile; it is the rug and towels that reflect the boy's love of trucks.

A teenager uses the room shown at top right. The wall-mounted sink features a stylish, round design that's echoed by the mirror. Towels hang conveniently on low, front-facing bars. Drawers and cabinets are inset, with easy-to-reach handles. For clear access to the room, the designer used pocket doors.

▶ NOTHING IN THIS TEEN BATH looks institutional, yet it is fully accessible. The sink serves well because there's legroom underneath and a faucet that's in easy reach. The adjustable mirror angles down for use from a seated position.

▲ GOOD-LOOKING BY ANY STANDARDS, this bathroom has wide clearances for wheelchair maneuverability. In the shower, the soap dish and faucet are together for convenient use from a chair. The tub faucet is opposite the half wall so it's not in the way when the wall is used for support.

Places to Play, Places to Study

Play areas and study areas have more in common than you might think. Both have a job to do, and both should be fun to use.

Every house needs territory where kids can feel free to do whatever strikes their fancy. A playroom's job is to be that kind of enabling environment. A playroom should be a friendly, lighthearted, and imaginative yet rugged place that invites kids to read, run, climb, paint, build, and make-believe. To do all that, the room needs good lighting, hardy surfaces, and an engaging mix of play stations. An expanse of open floor area, a kid-size table and seating, and ample, organized toy centers also make playrooms fun and welcoming.

Study areas, too, can be vibrant, imaginative spaces that children will enjoy using. Like playrooms, they should be comfortable and welcoming, but here the idea is to help children focus and concentrate. It's best to avoid elements that would be distracting, so separate the area from the phone, toys, and direct views into other rooms. A good homework center has excellent lighting; a comfortable, supportive chair; abundant, convenient storage for study supplies; and a desk and computer surface that are the right height for the child.

◀ A PEAKED DOORWAY creates a witty entrance to this dynamic and functional playroom. The abundant storage is a useful mix of clear-door cabinets, open shelving, drawers, and bins, allowing easy access to playthings while keeping the mess at bay. The central table, window seat, and chalkboard define various play areas, inspiring a healthy mix of activities.

Recreation Zones

KIDS EXERCISE THEIR INTELLECT AND IMAGINATION through indoor play, which helps prepare them for more formalized learning as they grow older. The most successful playrooms have activity zones that inspire children to participate in a wide range of activities.

Zones can be defined using built-ins and furniture groupings, floor finishes and carpeting, platforms and dropped ceilings, or color and pattern. Customize the zones to support the activity; for instance, quiet pastimes like reading or resting call for a soft, sheltered enclosure.

Kids can play games alone or with friends in a carpeted corner supplied with a bench, table, and game shelves. An open space with a hard floor or tight-weave, low-pile carpet is good for toy trucks, action figures, and blocks. Kids are most likely to do arts and crafts if little setup is required, so consider outfitting a spot with chalkboard or easel, a sturdy table that can handle spills, and a variety of art supplies.

▲ THOUGH TUCKED AROUND the perimeter to reserve floor area for active play, the zones in this playroom stand out because of their dynamic shapes and colors. Each area is distinctive, from the wavy snack bar to the stacked-box toy wall to the crafts center. Vinyl flooring makes a no-worry surface for the easel; the rest of the floor has soft, low-pile carpet.

▲ OPEN CABINETS FORM COLUMNS that organize toys and frame well-lighted art stations. For a clean look—and to place art supplies right where they are used—the center column has side-facing bins.

PLAY STATIONS pressed against the wall keep the floor clear but can be easily moved into action. The bright cabinet collage houses a rolling activity table, while art surfaces include a sliding chalkboard/display strip and a fold-back panel with corkboard on one side. Rollout toy carts are parked in color-coded garages.

▲ THE WINDOWED BULLETIN BOARD swings out from the wall, becoming a puppet theater or the wall of a make-believe house. The panel is mounted on a piano hinge, which is strong and unlikely to pinch fingers.

▶ THIS HOUSEBOAT PLAYHOUSE is surrounded by a harbor full of activity centers. The dock house in the background is a hideaway or puppet theater. The deck forms a curtained stage. Closets full of dress-up clothes and props flank the mirrored bench platform. Across the room are shelves of transparent toy bins and cabinets that hint at waterfront buildings.

◀ THE STURDY HOUSEBOAT, with operable shutters, steering wheel, and bell, rests on wheels so adults can move it to rearrange the room. Carpeting and fabric wall covering make a sound-insulated, cozy environment.

ART CENTRAL

▶ SPRIGHTLY IMAGES on the furniture stimulate kids to draw pictures of their own. That's easy for one or several kids to do, since the big chalkboard stretches across one wall and reaches almost to the floor. Each wall of the magical room is painted in one of the four furniture colors.

CHALKERBOARD ART WALL

A checkerboard of chalkboard and painted squares makes a decorative wall that's always changing.

The light squares are bright backdrops for framed or unframed art.

Chalkboard paint makes each black square a drawing surface.

Coated in gloss latex enamel, the light squares are easy to clean if chalk strays onto them.

Kids can "claim" their own chalkboard squares.

Closet Artistry

ARTS AND CRAFTS AREAS get messy fast, but with an art closet, you don't have to worry about it. Just close the doors on the clutter. This abundantly equipped art center fits into a 2-ft. by 5-ft. closet but can almost as easily be framed from scratch.

The closet is designed with convenience and easy maintenance in mind. Drawers, shelves, and a glide-out tabletop are finished in easy-care laminate. Doors hold a roll of art paper as well as a display panel and a smock hook.

Kids can either sit at the table or spread out their projects on the floor, which should, of course, be no-worry vinyl, tile, or poly-coated wood. Recessed can lights can be supplemented with track lighting outside the art center.

To make cleanup a habit, include a slim trash bin in a pull-out rack. If plumbing pipes are nearby, try to squeeze in a small sink for washing brushes, the tabletop, and paint-splattered hands.

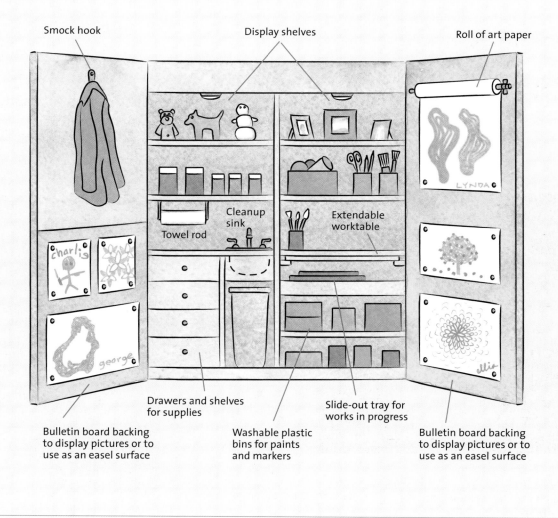

Smock hook

Display shelves

Roll of art paper

Towel rod

Cleanup sink

Extendable worktable

Drawers and shelves for supplies

Slide-out tray for works in progress

Bulletin board backing to display pictures or to use as an easel surface

Washable plastic bins for paints and markers

Bulletin board backing to display pictures or to use as an easel surface

Setting the Scene

IF YOU HAVE THE SPACE AND RESOURCES, consider going beyond the basic play area and creating a fantasy world—something that really inspires your child's imagination. Choose a central theme—something your kids love—and play with it. A few bold elements, such as wall murals, themed play structures, and toy boxes, can be enough to make an imaginary world come alive.

But why stop there? Integrate the room itself into the world of imaginary play. Turn built-ins into props and closets into extensions of the make-believe world, incorporating cabinets into a kitchen scene or disguising a window seat as a castle tower. Enrich the illusion with imaginative, removable embellishments attached to the wall. Need a shelf? Make it a propeller blade. Clothes hooks? Use horseshoes. Kids can really get into the swing of things when they interact with these thematic add-ons.

▲ THE LIFE-SIZE STREETSCAPE with faux open door and breeze-blown curtains is a vibrant backdrop that inspires make-believe play. An awning-style window valance and outdoor café table and chairs carry the scene into the room.

▶ IMAGINATIONS TAKE OFF in a room where art and reality meet. With its three-dimensional propeller, the painted biplane is ready to taxi down the carpeted runway into the room. A runway of vinyl flooring not only adds to the sense of a real airfield, it also makes a smooth and practical surface for rolling toys.

▲ PAINTING WHIMSICAL FLOWERS all around the room (even across the dresser!) makes this play space feel like a real garden. Bending the painted playhouse around the corner gives it houselike depth that fuels the imagination. The house even has a real door, which opens to a lighted walk-in closet-turned-house interior, with a faux window inside.

▶ AN INEXPENSIVE, easy-to-make "pig heaven," this room features fanciful wallpaper on the ceiling and around the chalkboard. The painted pig on the wall was modeled after a wallpaper pig, but a large wall appliqué or wallpaper mural would achieve a similar effect. The cow is papier-mâché. With the door removed and shelves installed, the closet becomes a media center.

10 Cool Ideas for Playrooms

- Hang rolls of art paper on the wall where the paper can be pulled down, or next to a table it can stretch across.
- Construct a multifunctional platform with toy cubbies or drawers underneath. Keep it flat or step it up two or three levels.
- Cover a wall panel with chalkboard or a dry-erase surface.
- Set up an arts and crafts corner with an easel, table and chairs, supply bins, and vinyl flooring.
- Keep toys visible but neat in clear plastic boxes.
- Organize toys in containers that can be brought out for play. Mount large containers on wheels; add rope handles to small containers.
- Provide a rolling table so that kits, crafts, and other works in progress can be put away.
- Wrap the walls in carpeting or fabric-covered soundboard where drawings can be tacked up.
- Attach hinged panels to the wall to add play options. Put a mirror on one side for dress-up. Or make a low window cutout and put a steering wheel on one side to make a bus or car.
- Use stacked cabinets to arrange toys by age level, with toddler toys on the bottom and smaller, more sophisticated playthings for older children on top.

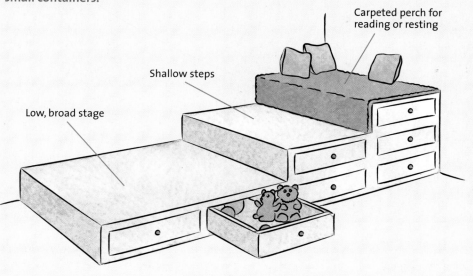

Carpeted perch for reading or resting

Shallow steps

Low, broad stage

Bonus Space

WHAT MAY LOOK LIKE UNUSABLE SPACE to you is exactly what kids like best. Odd, out-of-the-way nooks and crannies carry a certain magic, partly because they are one-of-a-kind and partly because their small size exclusively suits kids. The more self-sufficient these little spaces, the more appealing they are, so consider adding lighting or bookshelves.

Some of the best bonus spaces are over or under things—in places, that is, that have an air of secrecy. Good hideaway territory can be found under the eaves and under the stairs, in forgotten storage areas, and in never-used hollows behind walls. If no such bonus space exists in your house, you can create it. Add a loft to a closet. Build a railed platform with play space above and a cozy getaway below. As long as there is lighting, air, and enough headroom for them to sit comfortably inside, kids will enjoy the retreat for years.

▲ BIGGER IS BETTER for this storage block. Extending up and out from under the eaves, it recaptures a hefty chunk of wasted space and forms the platform for a cozy, curtained loft.

◄ THIS OUT-OF-THE-WAY CORNER is just right for an indoor fort. The chalkboard door to the room beneath will carry whatever messages the day's play requires. Scaling the climbing wall to the loft is an adventure in itself; kits and parts to build climbing walls are now widely available.

▲ JUST A FEW STEPS UP but sky-high in kid appeal, this reading nook has all the necessary comforts: a chaise and footrest for stretching out with a good book, natural lighting and well-placed lamps, and a soft rug. The bookcases create a sense of enclosure.

KID-SIZE GETAWAYS

► THIS COMPACT, cozy play corner is made all the more magical by the tiny Alice-in-Wonderland doorway that leads to adjoining play space. Kids have fun peeking through the little window and glass door; grownups can use the windows to keep an eye on things.

▼ LIGHTED, DRYWALLED, and softly carpeted, the cavity under the stairs makes an irresistible haven for kids. If there's room in such a place, add a tiny table and chairs and a shelf for books and small toys.

► THE SLOPED CEILING and closet walls in this attic carve out enticing play spaces. One is a cozy, sun-drenched corner; another is a tiny room—little more than a crawlspace—but the perfect secret escape for kids. The painted door adds to the sense of magic.

CHANGING AND GROWING

► VINYL MAKES A DURABLE PLAYROOM FLOOR, and glass turns the tabletop into an easy-care surface for art and snacks. But the room is equally appropriate for teens. The sporty patterns and colors are inviting for kids of all ages, as is the big window seat.

▼ AS THE KIDS GROW and their interests change, a room like this will keep up. The upholstered bench is good for naps and games now; its L-shape makes it a good place for older kids to hang out with friends. And the play table and toy shelves will transition into a homework center when the time comes.

Upstairs, Downstairs

T HE ONLY SPACE AVAILABLE for a playroom in your house may be down in the basement or up in the attic, where space is tight, headroom is limited, and light is scarce. Not to worry.

Attics and basements can make great play spaces, and their challenges frequently become opportunities to provide intimate, friendly surroundings for kids.

Here are the tricks: Tuck toy storage and play stations around the perimeter, lighting them individually and detailing them well to accentuate the variety of activities the room offers. Reserve as much open floor space as possible. In attics, use the low, angled ceilings to shape cozy, kid-size spaces. Build a dormer or pop in some roof windows to add light and height without major remodeling. In basements, light colors and good general lighting make up for the lack of windows. Carpet the walls as well as the floor, and the basement becomes a safe—and soundproof—place for kids to run around and let off steam.

◀ EVEN A SMALL DORMER or roof window improves an attic room. This one adds light, air, and a chalkboard niche. Though the window is operable, it is safe because it is high and opens only partway.

◄ THE FRESHNESS OF THE OUTDOORS
infuses this bright walk-out basement
play area, where structural columns are
disguised as trees and overhead duct-
work is enclosed in a cloudlike curved
soffit. Easy-maintenance vinyl paves the
art "patio." The grass-green carpet is a
durable, low-pile style.

▼ THE "TOWNHOUSES" in this basement play space serve several purposes:
They enliven the windowless room;
offer a backdrop for city-slicker make-
believe; form a whimsical environment
for a lighted couch/reading niche;
and provide abundant, inconspicuous
cabinets, drawers, and cubbies for
books and toys.

▲ WINDOWS, SKYLIGHTS, and electric lighting are well distributed around this room, leaving no murky corners and thus making every inch useful as play territory. The two-tone wall treatment with light color above de-emphasizes the angled panels and makes the room seem larger.

◀ NO NEED to rule out a windowless attic as a playroom location. Stacked roof windows were added to fill this attic with sunlight and fresh air. The shelving built into the knee walls makes excellent kid-size storage in space that would otherwise be wasted.

▼ IT'S SAFE FOR KIDS to roll and run in this sunny attic. A clear expanse of carpet covers the floor, and a gate with round-top pickets guards the stairway entrance.

BASEMENTS

▼ ◄ INSTALLING CURTAINS and building a raised floor at one end of the room sets the stage for children's performances. Kids draw the scenery in the art corner, and the rear wall of the stage is coated with magnetic paint so the scenery can be put up with magnets. With its smooth, laminated floor, the stage also could function as a tumbling area.

◄ WALLS WERE REMOVED from the basement to make way for a side-by-side playroom and family room. Complementary wood finishes and a string of molding connect the two spaces visually. Deep drawers hide toys, and the high desk rim keeps playroom-counter clutter out of view from the family room.

Recreation Space for Parents and Kids

WILL THE BASEMENT BE USED AS A PLAYROOM or as an exercise area? With some clever maneuvering, you can have both. It is not safe for small children to play around treadmills, exercise bikes, and other workout equipment, nor is it good to have toys scattered on the floor where adults will be exercising. The solution in this room is a partition with a window that gives adults and kids their own separate activity space while keeping the sense of togetherness intact.

The setup is a winner for both children and grown-ups. Young children can look through the window and enjoy the security of seeing their parents near-by. On the gym side of the glass, the exercise equipment can be arranged to let parents keep an eye on the kids—and extend a friendly wave—while burning calories.

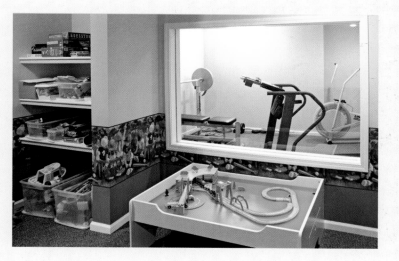

▲ IN THIS BASEMENT the exercise machines angle toward the corner so parents can watch the wall-hung television and supervise the kids. The window is mounted about 18 in. above floor level so it won't be hit by rolling toys or roughhousing kids.

Clutter Control

YOU CAN'T HAVE TOO MUCH STORAGE in a playroom. Using a mix of open and closed storage is the best strategy: Put favorite toys on shelves or in see-through bins where they can easily be seen, but keep the room from looking cluttered by enclosing other toys in labeled or color-coded cabinets, bins, baskets, and drawers. Young children can master a simple storage setup, and as kids get older, they can use a more elaborate storage system.

Store things where kids can reach them—and where they will use them. Blocks belong in bins near the floor, art supplies in divided drawers or cabinets in the craft area, dress-up clothes on a rod by a mirror or staging area. Reserve high cabinets for out-of-season equipment or for toys suitable only for older kids who share the space.

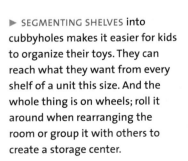

▶ SEGMENTING SHELVES **into cubbyholes makes it easier for kids to organize their toys. They can reach what they want from every shelf of a unit this size. And the whole thing is on wheels; roll it around when rearranging the room or group it with others to create a storage center.**

▼ VARIATIONS ON THE BASIC BOX—drawers and cabinets, shelves and pigeonholes—hold every kind of playroom paraphernalia here. The white laminate units are garnished with bands of open shelves that display just enough colorful toys. Lockable upper cabinets contain toys and movies unsuitable for toddlers.

TV CABINET ALTERATION

With a few additions, you can change an inexpensive or unfinished television cabinet or armoire into a compact station for kids' activities.

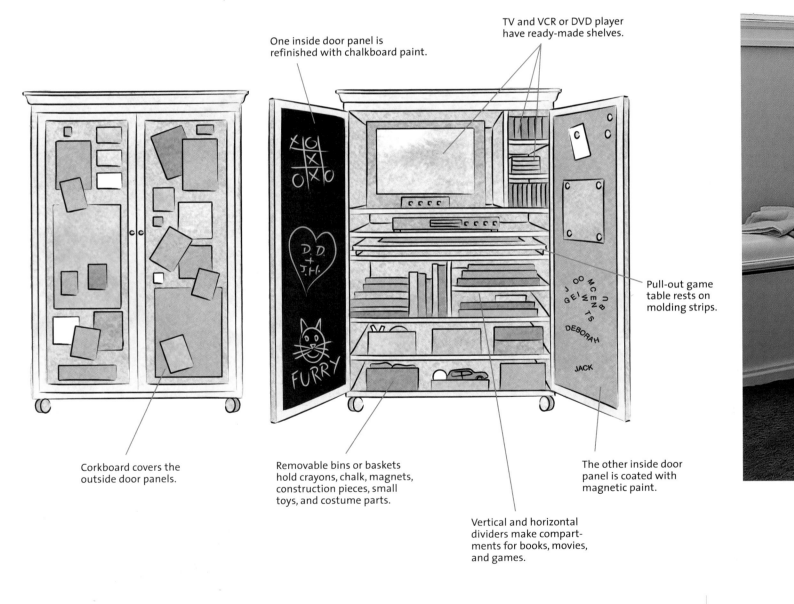

One inside door panel is refinished with chalkboard paint.

TV and VCR or DVD player have ready-made shelves.

Pull-out game table rests on molding strips.

Corkboard covers the outside door panels.

Removable bins or baskets hold crayons, chalk, magnets, construction pieces, small toys, and costume parts.

Vertical and horizontal dividers make compartments for books, movies, and games.

The other inside door panel is coated with magnetic paint.

◄ SIMPLE IN DESIGN but highly versatile, this sturdy wood wall unit has bins for books, toys, clothes, or shoes. In fact, another unit just like it is on the opposite wall of the walk-in closet. One contains toys and the other holds clothes; this simple system introduces kids to basic organizational concepts.

► JUST A FEW FEET of wall space is all you need for a slim rack like this. Sold as a plate rack, it works well as a place to stow or display toys, books, pictures, or collections where space is tight in kids' rooms.

STACKABLE STORAGE

▲ STACK THEM, sit on them, rearrange them—storage crates and cubes are inexpensive, strong, versatile containers that work in rooms for kids of any age. Customize the boxes with paint on the outside or inside, a fabric lining, or inserted dividers. A painted or laminated board across the top makes a smooth table surface.

◄ THESE DEEP, STACKABLE TOY BINS have wide openings but angled fronts so the contents are visible and accessible but unlikely to fall out. The dividers encourage kids to keep toys organized by type—blocks, books, games, and so on.

NEAT GAMES

◄ THIS ROLLING TABLE has big advantages. Kids can take it wherever they want to play. The tabletop is covered with textured sheets to support LEGO® structures. And unfinished construction projects—or masterpieces the kids are reluctant to disassemble—can be rolled out of the way.

▲ LURING KIDS into clutter control can be a great storage strategy: This biplane is so cool that its young pilot can't help but be motivated to keep the shelves neat. The nose of the plane is a door that drops down to reveal several storage compartments, while the door itself becomes a desk surface.

◄ PERFECT FOR KIDS who don't like dragging an armload of toys from the bin and carting them all back after playtime, these under-bench boxcars let them take the whole shebang. Kids roll a boxcar to where they are playing, use the toys, then drop them back in.

Homework Zones

DO YOUR HOMEWORK when designing kids' study space; with forethought, you can put together a homework center that will serve your kids well from first grade through high school. It can be lighthearted in terms of ambience (be careful not to make it overly distracting), but it should be equipped for serious work.

First, choose a location that's clearly separated from play zones. Wire the desk unit to exceed current power needs and allocate space for a computer and multiple electronic components, even if they are not going to be installed right away. Include easy-access shelving for books; ample, varied drawer space for desk supplies; and a desktop that is big enough for papers, books, and a computer keyboard. Provide good task lighting and supportive seating. Now, let the kids have fun adding their favorite colors, motifs, pictures, and accessories.

▼ A HALF WALL is just enough separation for kids' desks in shared or adjoining bedrooms. The computer equipment and wiring can be pooled, but the kids have their own work areas. They can talk and even peek over the wall, but they have enough privacy to concentrate on homework.

▲ SHELVES OR OPEN-FACED CABINETS over the desk establish a homework station where books and study materials are organized and in easy reach. Create a desktop or wall-mounted storage system with an arrangement of cubes, crisscross shelves, or funky yard-sale finds such as old suitcases.

▲ HIGH-TECH FINISHES partner well with computer equipment in a study area. Perforated metal sheets overlay the painted wall, forming a magnetic surface with a cool color background. The desk was smoothed with Bondo® and then coated with auto-body paint for durability and an industrial-strength gloss.

That Other Homework Zone: the Kitchen

DON'T BE SURPRISED if your kids prefer to do their homework in the kitchen. Young children in particular are most comfortable being near their parents around the house. That's especially true when they are doing schoolwork and want somebody close by to answer their questions.

Reserve one end of the counter as a homework place, perhaps adding a lower, desk-height section. Or install a desk in a kitchen corner where kids can sit without being in the way when you are fixing dinner. You can turn a spare closet into a computer station that works as a homework station for your kids as well as a command center for you. Wherever the kids sit, a few bookshelves and supply drawers should be handy.

Fit to Size

A HOMEWORK STATION that fits your child is a healthier, more comfortable, less tiring place to work. When she is in her desk chair, her back should be supported, and her legs should rest comfortably on the seat with knees bent and feet flat on the floor or footrest. Elbows by her sides, she should be able to use her keyboard and mouse without reaching out or bending her wrists.

For unstrained viewing, the computer monitor should be directly in front of her, away from glare, and about 18 in. to 22 in. from her head; its top edge should be at about forehead height. Task lighting should beam broadly from the sides.

Make the desk big enough to hold papers and books around the computer. Be sure to include a generous surface for noncomputer work, too.

▲ PRACTICAL IN EVERY WAY, this homework center is also wild and fun. An avid fish fan, the little boy helped with the design, specifying what fish to paint where. For now, a sheet of clear acrylic protects the desktop. When reference books replace the stuffed animals on the shelves, the desk will be ready.

▲ THIS WALL-MOUNTED STRUCTURE positions the desktop at a standard height but hangs off the floor to preserve play space. Stained wood shelves 18 in. deep can hold speakers, computer equipment and large books. If more holes are needed for wiring, they can easily be drilled into the slim shelves.

◄ WITH A BRIGHT FINISH and a mix of drawers, cabinets, and adjustable shelves, this built-in can evolve from toy center to desk. The cabinet fits a CPU tower, and the pencil drawer is a keyboard tray. Dresser drawers can be swapped for file drawers. Glass protects the desktop.

◀ THE BUILT-IN CLOSET with overhead soffit carves out space for a cozy little study corner. Inset drawers and desk-facing shelves capitalize on space against the angled wall. Though tucked away, the corner is brightened by a window, a recessed overhead fixture, and beams from a skylight.

◀ ARCHED MOLDING and wall-hung lamps make the homework zone look important and neatly separate it from the sleeping area. The shelving and practical double-wide desk are made of furniture-look built-ins that harmonize with the trim around the room.

▼ CORNER STRUCTURES capture a lot of useful space without intruding into the room. Different-sized drawers and cabinets in this unit accommodate a variety of essentials, from CDs to files and computer equipment. The deeply recessed center section fits the TV and monitor nicely. Though they're expensive, you can't beat the customized efficiency of built-ins.

▲ CONSTRUCTING CLOSETS at both ends of the wall did more than create storage space; it formed a niche just right for a desk and comfortable chair. The arched soffit lends intimacy to the mini-study. Bookcases are workable, but shallow enough to preserve the closet cavity.

Outdoor Play Spaces

WHEN THEY BURST OUT OF THE HOUSE on a sunny day, kids want to play with abandon. Whether they are in the mood for adventure or make-believe, your outdoor play territory should be ready to oblige.

The yard needs at least two components—an open, grassy area for games and running around and a safe, multipurpose play structure. The location of a play structure can add to its charm. Tuck a playhouse beneath a porch overhang, perch a fort on a sentry platform, or nestle a tree house in a cluster of big trees. If the yard has a slope to roll or run down, a cluster of shrubbery to use as a getaway, or some trees to climb or hide behind, so much the better. If not, a climbable play structure with a slide, enclosures, and lookouts will do the job.

Playhouses are the stuff of childhood memories. They can be elaborate dream houses or simple shelters. As long as they are big enough for a few kids (but small enough to exclude adults) and have some furnishings, they will be popular places for children to play house, have club meetings, or spend quiet time alone.

◄ EVERY CHILD LIKES CASTLES, and this 6-ft. by 8-ft. model is packed with features that invite adventure and imaginary play—kid-size doors, a lookout tower, a climbing wall, a private courtyard, and two rooms, one of them a secret space reached through a fake fireplace.

Dynamic Playhouses

A CHILD'S PLAYHOUSE IS HIS CASTLE. It's the place where kids rule and where they feel big and important. The structure should be small enough to exclude adults but big enough to accommodate children as they grow.

Make entering the house a thrill, using tiny openings reached via a ramp, ladder, bridge, or winding pathway. Include doors and windows, cabinets and shutters, mailboxes and peepholes that open and close. Distinctive features such as trap doors, rooms behind hidden doorways, and rope-mounted message buckets make a playhouse the pride of the neighborhood.

Children often know exactly what kind of playhouse they want. They may have a specific theme, location, or features in mind. Ask them to share their wish list, perhaps by drawing a sketch. Implement their ideas while using materials and colors that complement your house, and you'll have an imaginative structure that's as attractive to use as it is to behold.

▼ AS CHILDREN GO UP THE GANG-PLANK to this castlelike structure, they move into an imaginary world filled with play possibilities, from the lookout tower above to the "jail" with trapdoor access and rear exit. The decorative back of the porch bench is a bed backboard.

Retooling Existing Buildings

YOU MAY ALREADY HAVE THE MAKINGS of a play structure on your property. Reinvent a toolshed or garden hut as a playhouse by giving it a Dutch door, a low window or two, and flooring of wood, vinyl, or indoor-outdoor carpet.

Extra garage space may work as well. Wall off and insulate an area on the side of the garage, adding a little door and window for access and ventilation. If there's an unused attic corner overhead, install a ladder to give the garage "house" a loft.

The area under a sufficiently raised deck is fertile territory for a hideout enclosed with wood fencing. If space allows, add a platform or segment the playhouse into rooms connected by small doorways or peepholes.

▼ INSIDE THE COTTAGE the magic continues. Stained faux framing and white-painted, textured drywall mimic the look of an old-fashioned timber-frame house. The pine floor looks enchantingly rustic, too. The house has a nonworking stone fireplace and kid-size tables and chairs with tree-branch legs.

▲ MINIATURIZE ANY TYPE of structure, and it can become a magical play-house. This English cottage, just 230 sq. ft., has the diamond-pane windows, arch-top wood doors, rolled eaves, and steam-bent shingles of a fairy-tale house in the woods. The walls are stucco; the chimney is stucco stone.

▲ MUCH OF THE ALLURE of this four-room outpost is that its location, afloat on a slope in a wooded corner, speaks of adventure and secrecy. The deep overhang, high-railed balcony, and multiple entries—including "girls only" and "boys only" doors—equip the rustic cabin for clubhouse and play scenarios.

JUST LIKE HOME

▲ THIS TIDY LITTLE HOUSE with Dutch door and operable windows is irresistible for children. The covered front porch is just right for a couple of kid-size rocking chairs. The porch light and indoor fixtures make the house a fun place for parties or summer sleepovers.

◄ IT'S FUN TO PLAY HOUSE in this kitchen, which has real cabinets for cookware and dishes, a pretend refrigerator, and a fake stove with burners and big, turnable control knobs. The laminate flooring is durable, low-maintenance, and splinter-free.

▶ WITH OPERABLE WINDOWS and both front and back doors, this luxurious little place feels like a real house. Window bays add versatility to interior space. Pretty enough to dress up the backyard, the house also has its own fenced and gated yard for play space or a pint-size garden.

◀ THE CHARM of this garden getaway is that it is a tiny version of the main house, complete with picket fence and window boxes. The two-tiered interior is simple and open—big enough for young children to play or older kids to hang out.

UP, UP, AND AWAY

▼ BIG, CLUSTERED TREES make a broad base for this double-decker tree house. Trunks function as ladder rails at the base and as defining shapes to climb or play around within the house and on the deck. Another ladder, located inside the house, leads to the deck. Operable shutters protect the house from the elements.

▲ A FANCIFUL PAINT JOB raises the appeal of this elevated playhouse sky-high. Mounted on stilts, the plywood structure perches tantalizingly under overhanging branches, beckoning kids to climb up, peek out, and slide down.

▼ TO PROTECT THE GRAND, overhanging trees, this post-mounted house was built amid them but not attached to them. Designed as a preteen retreat, it has a steep, "adult-unfriendly" access ladder, a kid-size porch, and cable railings that ensure safety without blocking views.

▶ EXPOSED STUDS and sheathing give this house the rustic appeal of a clubhouse; the white walls and big, screened windows make it homey and comfortable. The preteen "homeowner" participated in the final stages of construction, specified the colors, and chose the furnishings and decor.

Active Outdoor Adventure

CHILDREN NEED TO TEST THEIR PHYSICAL LIMITS. Outside is the best place for this joyful experimentation, and an outdoor play structure should let kids stretch their skills in a safe, engaging environment.

The best structures stimulate kids' imaginations with appealing themes and varied play zones. Yet they are neutral enough to accommodate many solo and group activities and a wide range of make-believe worlds.

Create a self-contained play center or graft one onto trees or hills. Include multiple levels and platforms that become mini-destinations entered and exited via kid-size ladders, slides, ramps, bridges, grab bars, even climbing walls and zip lines. Incorporate a tunnel or steering wheel for toddlers, a climbing rope and tire swing for school-age children.

For soft landings, erect the structure over a 12-in.-deep bed of wood mulch or chips, sand, rubber mulch, or a surface of synthetic turf or rubber matting. If possible, position the structure where you can supervise from the house.

▼ KIDS PLAY OUT THEIR DREAMS of being firefighters—or just burn off extra energy—in this 9-ft. by 9-ft. brick and cedar firehouse. They can climb a ladder and slide down a fire pole inside or ring the tower bell and shoot down the spiral slide. A weather-proof coating covers the rooftop deck.

◄ SCREENED PLATFORMS branch out from this big tree, creating a draw for kids of all ages. Young children like the swings, the slide (made of polyurethane-coated signboard), and the cedar fort with climbing rope shooting out a trapdoor. Teens climb the wraparound tree stairs and relax in the fort.

◀ THOUGH PATCHED together with scrap lumber and inexpensive parts, this house is packed with play power—a plywood up-ramp, a slide, a crane rigged with rope-and-pulley bucket that's operated from inside the house, and a 20-ft. drain hose capped with plastic funnels for whispering messages. An acrylic topper turns the chimney into a skylight.

Lighthearted Landscaping

EVERY INCH OF THE YARD IS GAME for kids at play; bring out the fun with whimsical landscape elements. Create magical destinations by strategically placing bowers or paved patches in secret corners. Or frame small clearings with bushes, trelliswork, or wood fencing, and dot the encircling walls with tiny openings for "spying" or sending secret messages through.

Getting to these covert places can be half the adventure. Map a route that follows a winding path, perhaps one that slips under overhanging trelliswork and crosses a little bridge spanning an ivied depression, little pond, or rocky outcropping.

Fanciful features can be subtle enough to fit into sophisticated designs. Insert tiles of varied colors and shapes into the backyard terrace, forming creative patterns that double as games. Or use do-it-yourself paving pieces displaying your family's handprints, footprints, names, or artwork carved into tiles and then glazed.

▶ THIS HOPSCOTCH PATIO is a picturesque, easy-care landscape enhancement and a fun play surface. The cast concrete stepping stones, purchased at a home and garden store, are set in mortar over a concrete slab.

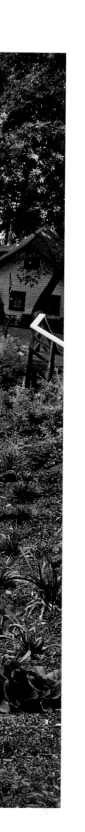

Sunken Treasure

JUST AS EVERY CHILD WANTS A BACKYARD TRAMPO-
LINE, every parent worries that his or her
kids will fall off the trampoline and get
hurt. Here's a solution: a trampoline at
ground level. This standard 12-ft.-diameter
trampoline nests in a 3-ft.-deep cavity with
grass all around and a buffer of surrounding
hay bales for good measure. Children love
jumping on the trampoline alone or with
friends, and a parent can jump aboard too,
delighting a small child by causing him or
her to rocket into the air.

The pit for this trampoline is reinforced
with a retaining wall of corrugated metal
and 12 symmetrically placed steel pipes. A
homemade jig pivoting on a central pipe was
used to make sure the pipes were positioned
properly. Compacted soil pads the space
between wall and tramp, while a redwood
rim forms a smooth and attractive border.

In areas with high precipitation, it's a good
idea to install a central drain under the trampoline or an underground pipe that funnels
water to a lower part of the yard.

▲ THIS TRAMPOLINE IS A POPULAR GATHERING PLACE where kids can enjoy a casual bounce or two, or work on
their gymnastics. The hay bales form a protective wall for young children and a launching platform for
older ones.

Credits

p. 2: (left) © Anice Hoachlander/ Hoachlander Davis Photography; Barnes Vanze Architects, Washington, DC; (right) © Brian Vanden Brink, Photographer 2004
p. 3: © James Carrier; Steven House, AIA, House + House Architects, San Francisco, CA

CHAPTER 1

p. 4: © 2002 Douglas A. Salin, www. Dougsalin.com; Linda Applewhite & Associates, San Rafael, CA
p. 5: © Andrea Rugg Photography; Christine L. Albertsson AIA, Albertsson Hansen Architecture, Ltd., Minneapolis, MN
p. 6 and 7: Photos courtesy Pi Smith/Smith & Vansant Architects, Norwich, VT; DPF Design, White River Junction, VT
p. 8: © Phillip H. Ennis Photography
p. 9: (top right and left) © Jessie Walker (bottom) © Robert Perron.
p. 10: © Allyson Jones, Wall Art Studio, Altadena, CA, www.allysonjonesmurals.com
p. 11: (top left) James Levine Photography, courtesy wallcandyarts.com; (top and bottom right) Photo courtesy Peggy Nelsen, www.thepaintedroom.com, Seattle, WA, 206-935-9009
p. 12: (top) Photo courtesy PoshTots, Posh-Tots.com
(bottom) © www.antongrassl.com; Leslie Saul & Associates, Inc., Cambridge, MA
p. 13: (top) © 2004 Chun Y. Lai; Edie Twining for Monastero & Associates, Inc., Cambridge, MA (bottom) © Christopher Covey Photography; Ellen Cantor, ASID, CID, Interior Consultant, Torrance, CA
p. 14: © John Umberger; Cynthia Florence Interiors, Allied ASID, Atlanta GA
p. 15: (top right and left) Photo courtesy Peggy Nelsen, www.thepaintedroom.com, Seattle, WA, 206-935-9009; (bottom) © 2004 Scott Rothwall Photography; Two's Company Interiors, Northridge, CA, for Lewis Homes
p. 16: © Jessie Walker
p. 17: © www.antongrassl.com; Leslie Saul & Associates, Inc., Cambridge, MA
p. 18: (top) © Mark Samu, Samu Studios Inc.; (bottom) © Alan Geller, San Francisco; Jeffrey O. Graham AIA, Graham Architects, San Francisco, CA
p. 19: © Laurence Taylor; Sharon Montanna Gilkey, ASID, Montanna & Associates, Orlando, FL
p. 20: © Tim Ebert; Kimberley Fiterman, Funtastic Interiors, Inc., New York, NY
pp. 20–21: Photo courtesy Kimberley Fiterman, ASID; Funtastic Interiors, Inc., New York, NY
p. 21: (top) © Laurence Taylor; Sharon Montanna Gilkey, ASID, Montanna & Associates, Orlando, FL; (bottom right) © Michael Mathers
p. 22: Photo courtesy Sageworks.com (Sageworks Decorative Painting)
p. 23: (top) © Bradley Olman; Jan Tomlinson, Roanoke, TX, Interiors by Decorating Den; (bottom) © Robb Miller; Two's Company Interiors, Northridge, CA, for Beazer Homes
pp. 24, 25: © Todd Caverly Photographer, Brian Vanden Brink Photos; Angela Caverly, Union, ME
p. 26: (top) © Brian Vanden Brink, Photographer 2004; (bottom) Photo by Jeff Heatley,

courtesy CRS Designs, Inc., New York, NY
p. 27: © Mark Samu, Samu Studios Inc.
p. 28: (top) © Bruce Campbell; Pine Cone Paths, Statesville, NC, pineconepaths.com; (middle) Photo courtesy Beth Lippert, Monkey Business LLC, Oshkosh, WI; (bottom) Photo courtesy The Land of Nod; www.landofnod.com
p. 29: (left) © Michael Mathers; (right) © Tria Giovan
p. 30: © Andrea Rugg Photography; Christine L. Albertsson AIA, Albertsson Hansen Architecture, Ltd., Minneapolis, MN
pp. 30–31: © Greg Hadley Photography; Brian and Kate Downs, Lucketts, VA
p. 31: Photo courtesy Georgia-Pacific Corp.
p. 32: (top) © Laurence Taylor; Sharon Montanna Gilkey, ASID, Montanna & Associates, Orlando, FL; (bottom) © 2004 Scott Rothwall Photography; Two's Company Interiors, Northridge, CA, for William Lyon Homes
p. 33: © Robert Mauer Photography; Builder: Benvenuti and Stein Inc., Evanston, IL
p. 34: © Philip Beaurline
p. 35: (top left) © Jessie Walker; (top right) © Robb Miller; Two's Company Interiors, Northridge, CA, for Trimark Pacific Homes; (bottom) © 2002 www.dougscott.com; Mithun Architects+Designers+Planners, Seattle, WA
p. 36: (top) © Allyson Jones; Allyson Jones, Wall Art Studio, Altadena, CA, www.allysonjonesmurals.com; (bottom) © 2004 Scott Rothwall Photography; Two's Company Interiors, Northridge, CA,for William Lyon Homes
p. 37: (top) © 2004 Scott Rothwall Photography; Two's Company Interiors, Northridge, CA, for William Lyon Homes; (bottom) © Exposures Unlimited/Ronald Kolb; Gary Lord, Prismatic Painting Studio, Cincinnati, OH, www.prismaticpainting.com
p. 38: © Alan Geller, San Francisco; Jeffrey O. Graham AIA, Graham Architects, San Francisco, CA
p. 39: Photo courtesy Michelle Rohrer-Lauer, Michelle's Interiors Ltd., Photo by Doug Hoffman, Studio West Ltd.
p. 40: Courtesy Georgia-Pacific Corp.
pp. 40–41: © Tim Street-Porter
p. 41: (top and bottom) Photo courtesy William Lesch Photography; Lori Carroll, ASID, IIDA, Lori Carroll & Associates, LLC, Tucson, AZ
p. 42: (top) © Phillip Jensen-Carter; Interior decorating by the Office of Carol J.W. Kurth AIA, Bedford, NY; (bottom) Jerry Blow Architectural Photography; Cari W. Jones, AIA, and Mark Jones, Raleigh, NC
p. 43: (top) © Anice Hoachlander/Hoachlander Davis Photography; Barnes Vanze Architects, Washington, D.C.; (bottom) Photo courtesy Pi Smith/Smith & Vansant Architects, Norwich, VT
p. 44: (top) Photo courtesy John Christian Anderson, Designer Laura Chasman; (bottom) © Tanglewood Design, playhouse designs.com; Photo by Skip Huntress
pp. 44–45: © Bud Harmon Photography; Cindy L. Nelson, ASID, CID, Interior Motives, Davis, CA
p. 45: (drawing) Barbara Ruys, AIA, San Diego, CA

p. 46: (top) © Laurence Taylor; Sharon Montanna Gilkey, ASID, Montanna & Associates, Orlando, FL; (bottom) © Polly Finlay
p. 47: © Laurence Taylor; Sharon Montanna Gilkey, ASID, Montanna & Associates, Orlando, FL
pp. 48–49: Photo courtesy Classic Remodeling & Construction, Charleston, SC
p. 49: (top) © Phillip H. Ennis Photography; Ferguson, Shamamian & Rattner, LLP, New York, NY; (bottom) Photo courtesy Contemporary Woodcrafts, Inc.; cabinets designed and manufactured by Contemporary Woodcrafts, Inc., Springfield, VA, www.cw-cabinet.com
p. 50: © Mark Samu, Samu Studios Inc.
p. 51: (top) Photo courtesy Robin Pruett Dent; Peggy G. Pruett, Allied ASID, of Cornucopia Designs, McDonough, GA; (bottom) © 2004 Scott Rothwall Photography; Two's Company Interiors, Northridge, CA, for William Lyon Homes
p. 52: Photo courtesy PoshTots, PoshTots.com
p. 53: (top) Photo courtesy Peggy G. Pruett, Allied ASID, Cornucopia Designs, McDonough, GA; (bottom) Interior design by Position by Design, Doug Handel photographer
p. 54: © Bradley Olman; Melissa Arnold, Interiors by Decorating Den
p. 55: (top) © Anne Gummerson Photography; (bottom left) © Robert Perron; (bottom right) Photo courtesy Wallies
p. 56: Photo courtesy Vibel, www.vibel.com
p. 57: Photos by Barry Dowe Photography
p. 58: (left) Photo courtesy Vibel, www.vibel.com; (right) © Tim Street-Porter
p. 59: (top) © Phillip H. Ennis Photography; Ferguson, Shamamian & Rattner, LLP, New York, NY; (bottom) © Robert Perron
p. 60: © 2004 Scott Rothwall Photography; Two's Company Interiors, Northridge, CA, for Lewis Homes
p. 61: (left) Photo and painting by Beth Gibson, Artist/Muralist, Ringgold, GA, 706-965-3589; (right) © David E. Durbak/ www.durbak.com; Theresa Bartolo, Allied ASID, Theresa Russell Interiors, Boca Raton, FL
p. 62: (top) Photo courtesy Stephen Smith Images; Jolayne Lyon Hawver ASID, Design Consultants Inc., Topeka, KS; (bottom left) © 2004 Scott Rothwall Photography; Two's Company Interiors, Northridge, CA, for Trimark Pacific Homes; (bottom right) © Straight Line Designs Inc., Photo by Stephen Nyran
p. 63: © Laurence Taylor; Sharon Montanna Gilkey, ASID, Montanna & Associates, Orlando, FL
p. 64: Photos © Virtually There; Karen Brown, Allied ASID, Karen Brown Interiors, Inc., Tampa, FL
p. 65: (top) © D. Randolph Foulds; Suzanne Price, Derwood, MD; Interiors by Decorating Den; (bottom) © Steve Vierra Photography
p. 66: © 2004 Chun Y. Lai; Edie Twining for Monastero & Associates, Inc., Cambridge, MA.
p. 67: (top) © Jessie Walker; (bottom and left center) © Michael Mathers
pp. 68–69: Photos courtesy Steven W. Cook; Steve Cook Architecture
p. 70: (top) © Thomas Sconyers, Photom Studios; Patricia Davis Brown, CKD, CBD,

Patricia Davis Brown Fine Cabinetry, Vero Beach, FL; (bottom) © Robb Miller; Two's Company Interiors, Northridge, CA, for John Laing Homes
p. 71: (top) Photo courtesy Vibel, www.vibel.com; (bottom) © Jessie Walker; Drawing by Michelle Rohrer-Lauer, Allied Member ASID, Michelle's Interiors Ltd., Grayslake, IL
p. 72: Drawing by Morris Stafford, AIA, The Loggia Group, PLLC, University Place, WA
p. 73: © Sandy Agrafiotis; Benjamin Nutter Associates, Architects, Topsfield, MA
p. 74: (top) Photo courtesy Vibel, www.vibel.com; (bottom left) Photo courtesy California Closets; (bottom right) © Tria Giovan
p. 75: (top) © Laurence Taylor; Sharon Montanna Gilkey, ASID, Montanna & Associates, Orlando, FL; (bottom) © Phillip H. Ennis Photography; Susan Steger Interior Design, Hewlett, NY
p. 76: (left) Photo courtesy York Wallcoverings; (right) davidduncanlivingston.com, © The Taunton Press, Inc.; Peter Breese, Vineyard Haven, MA
p. 77: (top) © Anice Hoachlander/Hoachlander Davis Photography; Barnes Vanze Architects, Washington, D.C.; (bottom) © Tria Giovan
p. 78: (top) © Tria Giovan; (bottom) © Robert Perron
p. 79: © Steve Vierra Photography
p. 80: (left top and bottom) © Jessie Walker; (top right) © Phillip H. Ennis Photography
p. 81: (top) © Andrea Rugg Photography; Christine L. Albertsson AIA, Albertsson Hansen Architecture, Ltd., Minneapolis, MN; (bottom) © Graham Architects; Jeffrey O. Graham AIA, Graham Architects, San Francisco, CA; Drawing by Murray Milne, Architect, Los Angeles, CA
p. 82: Photos © David Thomason; Cavalry Construction, Bedford, TX
p. 83: Drawing by Cari W. Jones, AIA, and Mark Jones, Raleigh, NC
p. 84: Photos © Taylor Dabney, Photographer; McGuire, Hearn & Toms, Manakin-Sabot, VA
p. 85: © Oscar Thompson; Marc-Michaels Interior Design, Winter Park, FL
p. 86: © Phillip H. Ennis Photography
p. 87: (top) © Brian Vanden Brink, Photographer 2004; (bottom) © Tria Giovan
p. 88: Photos © Tim Ebert; Esther Sadowsky, Charm & Whimsy, New York, NY
p. 89: (top) © Theresa Russell Interiors, Inc. Photo by Lucia Herrara; (bottom) © Tim Ebert; Esther Sadowsky, Charm & Whimsy, New York, NY
pp. 90–91: Photos Courtesy Vibel, www.vibel.com
p. 92: Photos courtesy California Closets
p. 93: Photos courtesy The Land of Nod

CHAPTER 2

p. 94: Charles Miller (*Fine Homebuilding* Kitchens & Baths, Winter 2002, p. 93); Renovation Innovations and Monkey-House Design, Portland, OR
p. 95: © John Rapetti/The Office of Carol J.W. Kurth, AIA, Architects
p. 96: (top) © Sargent 2002; Marc-Michaels Interior Design, Winter Park, FL; (bottom left) © Ken Gutmaker; (bottom right) Photo courtesy Charles Wilkins

p. 97: Photo courtesy York Wallcoverings
p. 98: (left) © Anice Hoachlander/Hoach-
lander Davis Photography; Barnes Vanze
Architects, Washington, D.C.; (right) © Tria
Giovan
p. 99: (top) © Steve Vierra Photography
(bottom) © John Rapetti; The Office of Carol J.W. Kurth, AIA, Architects
p. 100: Photos courtesy Wallies
p. 101: (top) James Levine Photography,
courtesy www.wallcandyarts.com (bottom
left) © 2002 Douglas A. Salin,
www.dougsalin.com; Sherry Scott, ASID,
CID, Design Lab, Redwood City, CA; (bottom right) © Michael Lyon; Hayslip Design
Associates, Dallas, TX
p. 102: (top) Photo courtesy Velux-America
Inc.; (bottom) © Andrea Rugg Photography; Christine L. Albertsson AIA, Albertsson
Hansen Architecture, Ltd., Minneapolis, MN
p. 104: (top) Photo courtesy Pi Smith;
Smith & Vansant Architects, Norwich, VT;
(bottom) © Philip Beaurline
p. 105: (top left) © Mark Samu, Samu Studios Inc.; (top right) Kate Coffey; Smith &
Vansant Architects, Norwich, VT; (bottom)
Courtesy York Wallcoverings
p. 106: © Graham Architects; Jeffrey O.
Graham, AIA, Graham Architects, San Fran-
cisco, CA
p. 107: (top) © Thomas Sconyers, Photom
Studios; Patricia Davis Brown, CKD, CBD,
Patricia Davis Brown Fine Cabinetry, Vero
Beach, FL; (bottom) © Anne Gummerson
Photography

CHAPTER 3
p. 108: © Greg Hursley/Through the
Lens Management; CG&S Design-Build,
Austin, TX
p. 109: © Graham Architects; Jeffrey O. Graham AIA, Graham Architects, San Francisco, CA
p. 111: © Leslie Wright Dow; The Bainbridge
Crew, Inc., Charlotte, NC
p. 110: Photo © Mark Samu, Samu Studios,
Inc.
p. 112: Photos © James Carrier; Steven
House, AIA, House + House Architects, San
Francisco, CA
p. 113: (bottom) © 2004 Chun Y. Lai; Edie
Twining, Monastero & Associates, Inc.,
Cambridge, MA
p. 114: Photo courtesy Sageworks.com
(Sageworks Decorative Painting); Drawing
by Brenda Gartman, Gartman Custom
Works of Art, Shelburne, VT
p. 115: Drawing by Laura Birns, ASID, Laura
Birns Design, Del Mar, CA
p. 116: (top) © Bradley Olman; Bonnie
Pressley, Allied ASID, Benbrook, TX, Interi-
ors by Decorating Den; (bottom) © Virtual-
ly There; Karen Brown, Allied ASID, Karen
Brown Interiors, Inc., Tampa, FL
p. 117: (top) Interior design by Position By
Design, Doug Handel photographer; (bottom) © Michael Pennello Photography;
Mary C. Strickland and Bea Hopkins, Residential Design Concepts LLC, Virginia
Beach, VA
p. 118: (top) © Tria Giovan; (bottom) © Ken
Gutmaker
p. 119: © Peter Krupenye; The Office of
Carol J.W. Kurth AIA, Bedford, NY
p. 120: (top right) © Robert Perron;

(bottom right) Photo courtesy Karie B. Cal-
houn & Joyce Cerato; (left) © Barbara Bois-
sevain Photography
p. 121: (top) © Tria Giovan; (bottom) © Nor-
man McGrath
p. 122: Photo courtesy Velux-America Inc.
p. 123: (top) © Greg Premru; LDa Architects,
Cambridge, MA; (bottom) Photo courtesy
Michelle Rohrer-Lauer, Michelle's Interiors
Ltd., Photo by Barry Dowe Photography
p. 124: Photo courtesy Velux-America Inc.
p. 125: (top) Photo courtesy Velux-America
Inc.; (bottom) © Tria Giovan
p. 126: Photo courtesy Alain Jaramillo,
© Case Design/Remodeling, Inc.; Jim
Crenca, Case Design/Remodeling, Inc.,
Bethesda, MD
p. 127: (top) © Peter Vanderwarker; LDa Architects, Cambridge, MA; (bottom) © Rick
Hammer, Designer: Department of Interiors, LTD., www.deptofinteriors.com
p. 128: Photo courtesy Maine Cottage,
Dennis Welsh, photographer
p. 129: © John Gillan; Marc-Michaels Interi-
or Design, Winter Park, FL
p. 131: (left) © Sargent 2002; Marc-Michaels
Interior Design, Winter Park, FL; (right)
© John Umberger; Cynthia Florence Interiors, Allied ASID, Atlanta, GA
p. 132: (top) Photo courtesy York Wallcoverings; (bottom) Photo courtesy The Land of
Nod
p. 133: (top right)© 2002 Michael C. Snell;
Jolayne Lyon Hawver ASID, Design Consultants Inc., Greg Inkmann, Topeka, KS; (top
left) © James Carrier; Steven House, AIA,
House + House Architects, San Francisco,
CA; (bottom left) Photo courtesy Michelle
Rohrer-Lauer, Michelle's Interiors Ltd., Photo
by Barry Dowe Photography;
p. 134: (top) Photo courtesy Maine Cottage,
Dennis Welsh, photographer; (bottom)
© The Gallick Corporation, Design/Build
Contractor, Photo by Woody Cady Photog-
raphy.
p. 135: © Kathy Detwiler, Designer: Jennifer
Mitchell, Jennifer Mitchell Design, Grosse
Pointe Farms, MI
p. 136: Photo courtesy Sageworks.com
(Sageworks Decorative Painting); Terry
Terry Design, Dallas, TX
p. 137: (top) © Elisabeth Groh; Barbara E.
Hafften Allied ASID, Barbara Hafften Interior Design, Chisago City, MN, Brian
Amundson, Mother Hubbards Cupboards,
Hager City, WI (bottom) Photo courtesy
Contemporary Woodcrafts, Inc., Cabinets
designed and manufactured by Contemporary Woodcrafts, Inc., Springfield, VA;
www.cwcabinet.com
p. 138: Photo courtesy Pi Smith; Smith &
Vansant Architects, Norwich, VT
p. 139: (top left) © Phillip H. Ennis Photography; Ferguson, Shamamian & Rattner,
LLP, New York, NY (bottom left) Photo courtesy Michelle Rohrer-Lauer, Michelle's Interiors Ltd. Photo by Doug Hoffman, Studio
West Ltd; (right) © Phillip H. Ennis Photography; Ferguson, Shamamian & Rattner,
LLP, New York, NY

CHAPTER 4
p. 140: Photo courtesy PoshTots, Posh-
Tots.com
p. 141: Photo courtesy La Petite Maison,
lapetitemaison.com

p. 142: Photo courtesy Katelynscastles
p. 143: (top left) © 2003 Keenan Ward;
Robert Mahrer General Contractor Inc.,
Santa Cruz, CA; (top right) © 2003 Keenan
Ward; Robert Mahrer General Contractor
Inc., Santa Cruz, CA; (bottom) Photo courtesy Katelynscastles
p. 144: © Anderson-Moore Builders, Inc.
Photos by Sharon Haege, Brick House Creative; Anderson-Moore Builders, Inc., Win-
ston-Salem, NC
p. 145: (top) Photo courtesy La Petite
Maison, lapetitemaison.com; (bottom)
© Robert Perron
p. 146: (left) Photo courtesy Mark IV
Builders, Inc., Photo by Woody Cady Photography; (right) © Allyson Jones; Allyson
Jones, Wall Art Studio, Altadena, CA,
www.allysonjonesmurals.com
p. 147: (top and bottom) © Andrea Rugg
Photography; Christine L. Albertsson AIA,
Albertsson Hansen Architecture, Ltd., Minneapolis, MN
p. 148: (left) © Randy Brown Architects.
com; (right) Photo courtesy Timothy Rice,
Assoc. AIA, on behalf of the American
Heart Association, MN
p. 149: © 2003 Feinknopf Photography;
Richard Taylor, AIA, Richard Taylor Architects, LLC, Dublin, OH
p. 150: © NAI Architecture/Planning/Interi-
ors; William K. Mayfield, AIA, NAI Architec-
ture/Planning/Interiors, Mount Hermon, CA
p. 151: Photo courtesy Thomas L. Chamber-
lain, AIA, San Jose, CA

For More Great Design Ideas, Look for These and Other Taunton Press Books wherever Books are Sold.

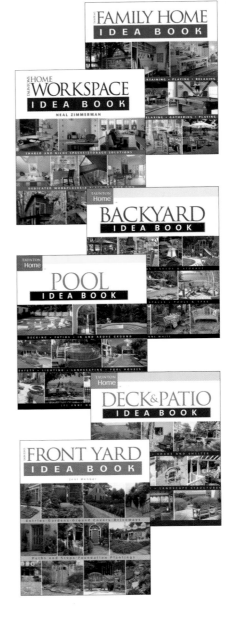

NEW KITCHEN
IDEA BOOK
ISBN 1-56158-693-5
Product #070773
$19.95 U.S.
$27.95 Canada

NEW BATHROOM
IDEA BOOK
ISBN 1-56158-692-7
Product #070774
$19.95 U.S.
$27.95 Canada

TRIM IDEA BOOK
ISBN 1-56158-710-9
Product #070786
$19.95 U.S.
$27.95 Canada

TAUNTON'S
HOME STORAGE
IDEA BOOK
ISBN 1-56158-676-5
Product #070758
$19.95 U.S.
$27.95 Canada

NEW BUILT-INS
IDEA BOOK
ISBN 1-56158-673-0
Product #070755
$19.95 U.S.
$27.95 Canada

TILE IDEA BOOK
ISBN 1-56158-709-5
Product #070785
$19.95 U.S.
$27.95 Canada

TAUNTON'S
FAMILY HOME
IDEA BOOK
ISBN 1-56158-729-X
Product #070789
$19.95 U.S.
$27.95 Canada

TAUNTON'S HOME
WORKSPACE
IDEA BOOK
ISBN 1-56158-701-X
Product #070783
$19.95 U.S.
$27.95 Canada

BACKYARD
IDEA BOOK
ISBN 1-56158-667-6
Product #070749
$19.95 U.S.
$27.95 Canada

POOL IDEA BOOK
ISBN 1-56158-764-8
Product #070825
$19.95 U.S.
$27.95 Canada

DECK & PATIO
IDEA BOOK
ISBN 1-56158-639-0
Product #070718
$19.95 U.S.
$27.95 Canada

TAUNTON'S
FRONT YARD
IDEA BOOK
ISBN 1-56158-519-X
Product #070621
$19.95 U.S.
$27.95 Canada